Julie – Enjoy this book – I've removed all the calories! Always remember to preserve the goodness of your great fan

Dr. John
11/23/05

Sweetness Preserved

THE STORY OF THE

Crown Candy Kitchen

By Dr. John L. Oldani, PhD

Virginia Publishing

SWEETNESS PRESERVED: *The Story of the Crown Candy Kitchen*

©2005 John Oldani, Ph.D.

Virginia Publishing Company

P.O. Box 4538, St. Louis Missouri 63108   t: 314-367-6612

www.stl-books.com

Book cover and interior design: ©2005 Michael Kilfoy

Design assistance by Evelyn Gwi

Studio X, St. Louis, Missouri   t: 314-773-9989

www.studiox.us

ISBN: 1-891442-34-1

Library of Congress Control Number: 2005924783

Edited by Fran Levy and Julie Stevenson

Printed in USA

Field of Dreams Quote: ©2005 by Universal Studios Licensing LLLP.
Courtesy of Universal Studios Licensing LLLP. All Rights Reserved.

All rights reserved. No part of this book may be reproduced in any form or by any electronic or mechanical means, including information storage and retrieval systems, without permission in writing from the author or publisher, except by a reviewer, who may quote brief passages in review.

"This field, this game. It's part of our past, Ray.
It reminds us of all that once was good
and it could be again."

FROM THE MOVIE: "Field of Dreams"

DEDICATION

To my mother and my muse, *Mary Knez Oldani,* who truly understands the immigrant experience and lovingly shared it with me over the decades of oral traditions, I am deeply grateful for all that you are and all that you have done. In some way, unknown to me, I am sure you will understand and appreciate this book.
ZBOGOM!

To *George Karandzieff,* who died on Easter Sunday, March 27, 2005, as this story of his business was completed for publication. George died from complications of Parkinson's disease, which he fought, characteristically, for several years. He granted me hours of interviews over more than two years. In addition to the confectionery business, I learned as much about what it means to be a human being. "Remember," he told me, "we only go around one time; make your mark as a person, not a businessman, who makes a difference."
He will be missed!

Photos, photo illustrations on pages 3, 7, 14, 22-23 center, 32, 34, 35, 36 left and right, 37 left, 38, 48 left, 49 right, 52, 53, 62, 63, 64 left, 71, 84, 85, 86, 87, 90, 93, 94, 95, 96, 100, 101, 102
©2005 John George Frangoulis

Photos on pages 10-11, 16, 20, 21, 22, 37 right, 39, 43, 51 left, 51 right, 54, 56, 58, 61, 69, 81, 88, 89, 91, 98, 99, 104:
©2005 Chris Heuer

Photos on pages 97, 193 courtesy of Craig Mold

Photo on pages 111 ©2005 Angela Key

Photos on pages 23, 44 ©2005 John L. Oldani

Photos on cover and pages 33, 55, 57 ©2005 Michael Kilfoy

Photoediting and retouching: Michael Kilfoy

All other photos courtesy of the Karandzieff Family

TABLE OF CONTENTS

INTRODUCTION BY FRANK CUSUMANO	12
PREFACE	15
ACKNOWLEDGMENTS	18
CHAPTER 1: *Just a Place*	21
CHAPTER 2: *The Beginnings:* FROM MACEDONIA TO ST. LOUIS	25
CHAPTER 3: *Developing a Brand*	33
CHAPTER 4: *The Tradition Must Continue*	39
CHAPTER 5: *The Supporting Cast:* LEARNING A RITUAL	47
CHAPTER 6: *The Folklore:* DEVELOPED ORAL TRADITIONS	53
CHAPTER 7: *A Paparazzi Paradise!*	71
CHAPTER 8: *Some Sweet Stats:* 8 TONS OF CHOCOLATE, PLUS	85
CHAPTER 9: *Crown Candy Recipes*	89
CHAPTER 10: *Curious Queries and More!*	95
AFTERWORD: *How Long Can Sweetness Be Preserved?*	101
APPENDIX: SURVEY BY THE UNIVERSITY OF MISSOURI AT ST. LOUIS	105
INDEX	108

Intro by Frank Cusumano

As the father of three, my goal in life is not to be the best television sports anchor or radio talk show host, but to entertain my kids as often as possible. And when your children have met Brett Hull, Jim Edmonds and Annika Sorenstam before they were 10, sometimes it's tough to interest them in everyday things. However, one place in St. Louis never fails: Crown Candy Kitchen!

As soon as we arrive, we go directly to the back of the place. George is always there. His hands are always right in the middle of the chocolate. And he immediately gives you a warm greeting and pulls his hand out of the chocolate as if to shake it. You are actually about to shake it before you realize how foolish you are about to look and you politely nod while George laughs.

Then George offers us anything we want. You have never seen three kids move so adroitly. It's as if they had been on the "Subway diet" and had not ever gone trick-or-treating in their lives. After five minutes, we leave the back room with three children bouncing off the walls, faces covered in chocolate.

Crown Candy is very similar in a sense to my family's background. Our restaurant, Kemoll's, was just like it: a candy kitchen with wonderful homemade chocolates and tasty sandwiches. When my father married into the Kemoll family, he changed the theme of the restaurant to make it an elegant destination for St. Louis patrons. But when you look at the early pictures of Kemoll's, you feel like you are looking at Crown Candy as it is today — and, in fact, as it was more than 90 years ago.

INTRODUCTION: by Frank Cusumano

Crown Candy fits my definition of a "joint," with its stainless steel milkshake containers, malt glasses, wooden booths, and all the old Coca-Cola signs. Sometimes I feel like I should drive there in a 1965 Mustang. But what makes it special — what sets it apart — is the food. I can honestly say I have never tasted anything in that place that hasn't been superb.

Dr. Oldani has captured the vision of Crown Candy Kitchen. It hasn't changed since it opened in 1913 — thank God! It is needed as a reminder of what fun, family, joy and childhood used to be. Throughout this book are photos and descriptions of a family that has been committed to its mission for the business. There have been numerous opportunities — even "begging" offers — to start other Crown Candy Kitchens in various areas around St. Louis, even at some malls. But, fortunately, the Karandzieffs have resisted all of them in order to maintain their "truth." Reading the stories of Grandfather Harry and Uncle Pete, the "characters" who have been regulars at Crown, and even the real questions that customers have asked over the years, will give you not only a sense of St. Louis history, but a clue as to what "Americana" is all about.

Read this story of an American institution before you visit Crown Candy Kitchen for the first time, or before you visit it again. And be sure to bring the kids! ♛

Preface

There's an old American superstition about birth that, with variations, tells us that a pregnant woman may be so frightened by something, or, conversely, so attracted to something, that the baby will have some birthmark that "resembles" the mother's attraction or revulsion during her pregnancy. And countless "folk" show birthmarks that look like deer, rabbits, skunks, or snakes as things that frightened their pregnant mothers. One's imagination gets a real test here.

Rarely are there "signs" of attractions. Perhaps Americans love the macabre. But if the old wives' tale is true, there should be a birthmark somewhere on my person that resembles a chocolate ice cream sundae. You see, that covers both ice cream and chocolate — both are undeniably part of my genetic makeup. And I know my mother loves both of them as much as her children, but she never mentioned an unusual craving during her pregnancies. In fact, I know she was as fanatic about candy and ice cream at 80 years old as she was at 30. So was my father, by the way — enough of this superstition!

The combination of both parents' enthusiastic love of ice cream and candy is wrapped up in their comically and optimistically spoken epigram: "Life is too short. Eat dessert first." My brother, sister, and I never had a chance! A work ethic was important, as was education, a love of God, family, and friends, but they could all be appreciated more with the addition of ice cream and candy.

Our freezer never operated properly unless it had some ice cream in it. Usually, there were several gallons,

Valentine's Day is always a beautiful pageant at the Crown Candy Kitchen.

mostly chocolate, but always one new flavor "in case one's ice cream cravings changed." Since my father managed a grocery store, these desserts were in closer proximity, much more tempting, and as easily carried home as the evening paper. This may explain their ubiquity; I don't know. And I really don't care; I'm just glad my parents had these "sweet" habits. Of course, over the past decade or so, I have noticed my body displaying the telltale signs of my love for chocolate candy or spumoni ice cream, but as I told you, life is too short….

Even if the ice cream was not in our freezer or the candy in the pantry, there were "ways" to get it. My father grew up on The Hill, the Italian section in southwest St. Louis. But, as an adult, he moved to an area in northwest St. Louis, known as Walnut Park, where he managed my uncle's (his brother's) grocery store. And, in North St. Louis, we were not far from Crown Candy Kitchen. Are you starting to get the picture?

Usually on Sundays, for special treats (as if ice cream and candy being always available were not enough) we would be taken to Crown Candy for sundaes or malts or chocolate ice cream sodas — if we had been particularly good that week, both in school and at home. So began my attraction to the wonders of what the Karandzieff family had done since 1913.

The Coca-Cola memorabilia all around the store was my favorite memory. It was fun just to look at all the faces on the serving trays and wonder. The juke box was filled with songs of the day and I could pick the one I wanted to hear without waiting for it on the radio. The candy case had homemade taffy — very soft and flavorful and wrapped in that silky waxed paper. The chocolate covered pecans — I didn't like them then, but crave them now — were sitting in covered trays on top of the candy case. There were jawbreakers and licorice pieces; chocolate marshmallows and caramels; even broken milk chocolate and chocolate-covered raisins. And all of them were very good!

PREFACE

And genially greeting us, almost every time, was "some man from the store" whom I didn't know then, but have since learned was either Harry Karandzieff, the founder of Crown Candy, Uncle Pete, or later, George Karandzieff. It was George whom I came to know best after I grew up and visited Crown with my friends. He was the natural promoter, marketer, and always cheerful greeter. I never forgot his quick smile and easy laugh, delivered with a piece of candy.

As an undergraduate and graduate student at Saint Louis University, it was a quick trip for us down St. Louis Avenue to visit Crown Candy. In some stressful period during my studies, I usually found myself at Crown Candy needing the comfort of that chocolate malt or banana split. It worked and I didn't even wonder why.

When I served as a consultant to corporate St. Louis, primarily in the downtown area, Crown Candy still remained a weekly luncheon spot. I always took our secretaries there on Secretary's Day or my boss on Boss's Day. It was, and is, a natural and inviting place to forget problems of the work world.

It was in those later years, as a professor and consultant, that the idea of this book came to me and to Andy Karandzieff, George's son. Andy and I had gotten to know each other from my weekly visits and "same booth mentality." Eventually, Andy learned of my 25 years of experience as a guest on KMOX radio and as writer for Johnny Cash's radio program, "American Folklore." The idea for a book about the history of Crown Candy Kitchen simply emerged from our conversations.

What I am presenting in this book has been for me a labor of love. My own history has come full circle. Crown Candy Kitchen is the same place it was when I first saw it. It has meant something different to me at every stage of my life. And my "genetic" love of ice cream and candy has some meaning, finally!

So this manuscript is about a family and a business. But it is more than that. I hope you will see the American Dream and the Melting Pot and the need for vision, pride, consistency, comfort, and, most of all, innocence, in our hectic lives. And I hope you will visit and taste the ice cream, candies, and lunches and sit in those booths full of stories, and that you, also, will find some meaning. ♛

Acknowledgments

It often appears trite when an author thanks those people who have helped in the writing of a book. And a listing of supporters certainly cannot include all who contributed ideas, memories, or suggestions. But I am sincerely grateful to the following people:

The Karandzieff Family — George, Bessie, Mike, Tommy, and Andy — have been as generous as their ice cream creations. They are special, humble people who have created a legend in St. Louis without fanfare, simply by caring.

The employees of Crown Candy Kitchen have encouraged me every step of the way. Bonnie Brogan, a long-time waitress at Crown, who died during the writing of this book, pushed me in directions I never considered. She was open, caring and dedicated, working long hours while suffering quietly.

Tammy Siebels, Pam Mardirosian and Denice Chaffin, who, with their work ethic and dedication, have shown and told me more than their words could ever do. And to Donnie Stevens, Todd Goebel, Joe and Max Eisenbraun, Nicki and Natalie Kranz, Dennis Horan and Lawrence Ross, who have helped by listening to me and for me, I am very grateful.

To the St. Louis media people who not only frequent Crown Candy but also pushed me so that this work would be undertaken, I am thankful: Joe Pollack, Anne Lemons, Kent Ehrhardt, Tim Dorsey, Frank Cusumano, Dick Ford, Deb Peterson, Jennifer Blome, Tim Ezell, Steve Savard, Mike Owens, Ron Elz, Martin Duggan and Al Wiman.

Governor Bob Holden; the Honorable Tom Villa; Chief of Police, Joe Mokwa; Fire Chief, Neil Svetanics; quintessential restaurateur, Vince Bommarito; "Mr. St. Louis," Joe Edwards; UMSL professors Andrew Hurley and Will Winter; Susan Tschetter of Landmarks St. Louis; publisher Steve DeBellis; and Joan Fann of the St. Louis Symphony — I will not forget your support.

ACKNOWLEDGMENTS

Family and friends: Tina Thompson; Craig Mold; Fannie Otso Buth, and her mother, Zyo Otso; Patricia Kallaos; Socrates Dendrinellis; Bill Fellenz; and Steve Marx, for completing the facts and offering direction, I am very appreciative.

To David and Janine Potrzeboski; Bill Harrison; Judy Holmes; Doris Reeves; and Bob Morris — long-time customers who inspired me through their enthusiasm — a grateful thank you.

Thanks to Todd Morris, President of Candy Crate, Inc. (www.candycrate.com) and to The International Ice Cream Association for their interesting facts about candy and ice cream.

To John Frangoulis, who took many of the pictures I requested and who was as passionate about the work as I was, I am grateful beyond words for the time he took away from his career, and especially for his artist's eye.

To Scott Shy, a superior graphic artist, who suggested more ideas than I can recount and prayed for my success, I am very indebted.

I can never repay Chris Heuer, for whom, in a very real sense, I owe the publication of this book — his imaginative approaches, his photography expertise, but mostly, his friendship.

Jeff Fister, my publisher, and Michael Kilfoy and Evelyn Gwi, my book designers: I am most appreciative of their patient education in the art of producing a book and for encouraging me throughout the process. They are a class act! And to Whitney Haas for reading a very early draft of the manuscript, and Kathy Lass and Jim Dowd for listening, I am very thankful.

Thanks to my brother, Bud (Charles) for his cheerleading and constant encouragement.

To my sister, Mary (Micki) Bisesi, and my niece, Angela Bisesi Key, and her children, Dominic and Adam, for their publicizing of my work, the mystery visits to Crown Candy, and their critical everyday opinions — thank you very much. You will all have giant jawbreakers for life!

Thanks to A. Charles Oldani, my father, to Steve and Tony Bisesi, and to Don Donley, who never left my writer's brain during this whole composition. Somehow I'll make certain you get a copy of this book.

My most heartfelt thanks to my family: Carollee, my wife, who kept me focused with her positive encouragement, endured my ugly manifestations of writer's block, and never complained when I spilled chocolate sauce on my white shirt, I can never give you enough thanks; my children, Matt, Susan Oldani Hendrickson, and David, and their spouses, Jennifer, Joe, and Monica, who took my negative thoughts and worries and made them positive, and who sampled all the candies and never complained about the carbs or the potential weight gain — you are appreciated very much; Gemma and Josie, who, when they read this book some day, will know a bit more about their grandfather, and, I hope, be pleased. ♛

Sweetness Preserved: THE STORY OF THE CROWN CANDY KITCHEN

Just a Place

It's just a place, like any other. It's a room with four walls, one of which is a half-sized store-front window. If you look up, you'll see an undistinguished tin ceiling. The booths are wooden: 10 along the walls, and six smaller ones in the center. Fifty-two people can be seated if you add chairs at the end of each of the larger booths. This place is not selling comfort.

There are two doors at the entrance. One leads to a very small foyer and the other opens to those 16 booths. Entering this second door, your eye might be directed to the large jukebox at the end of the six small middle booths, centered on green-white tiles that cover the floor. Or you might be gazing at the old wooden candy case to your left. It's not very large, but it's filled with handmade chocolate specialties, molded chocolate treats, rock candy, horehound drops, licorice — red or black — and gigantic jawbreakers.

If you look directly to the left of the candy case, you'll see the soda fountain, its countertop abundant with chocolate-covered Oreos and packs of gum — including the long-forgotten Black Jack. On the wall behind the counter is a large mirror, and in its reflection are the malt machine and rows of tulip-shaped ice cream sundae bowls. Unseen except for the bobbing head of the soda jerk are containers filled with ice cream — 14% butterfat — in 12 different flavors.

You won't notice the color of the walls because they are covered with Coca-Cola trays: no reproductions — only the real thing in this place. You'll even see posters of the Coca-Cola ladies from another era, and one of '50s crooner Eddie Fisher, toasting you with a Coke as he sings.

The Fire Chief Special Sundae could make you heavier just by looking at it!

Sweetness Preserved: THE STORY OF THE CROWN CANDY KITCHEN

The 24-ounce chocolate malt is the biggest seller among the ice cream specialties. Can you drink 5 of them in 30 minutes?

The antique ice cream flavor board, which rarely changes. Don't look for the flavor of the month here!

But the most perfect, real, interesting vision for you happens only when you close your eyes. You'll hear your grandfather, or your great-grandfather, or perhaps your parents ordering a phosphate, a chocolate banana malt, a BLT on white toast — maybe a chocolate soda with two straws, or a hot fudge sundae with homemade fudge sauce. You hear the ghosts of the past planning a date for a prom, proposing marriage, or asking questions of the soldiers who are home on leave. You will not hear conversations about diets, carbs or obesity.

You are living history without the forced reconstruction of a well-intentioned historical society or a docent striving so enthusiastically to help you relive the past. Those booths you sit in; the glass cases you see; the candy molds on display; that malt machine ..... Everything is the same as it was in 1913 when The Place opened its doors. The same family operates The Place, using the same recipes and even the same candy molds.

"If these walls could talk:" that's not a cliché for Crown Candy Kitchen. It has been here nearly a century: a time that has seen two world wars; 13 U.S. presidents; The Vote for women; gas stoves and microwaves; electric typewriters and personal computers; pogo sticks and X-Boxes; Metrecal and Atkins; the Charleston and Hip-Hop; propeller planes and the Concorde. Crown Candy Kitchen witnessed all of these, survived many of them, and became a place where they could be discussed.

INTRODUCTION: *Just a Place*

Some treasures of nostalgia from the Karandzieff Family's Coca-Cola collection.

It is a "place," to be sure, but, more important, it is a living character that remained steady in its vision, certain of its tradition, flourishing and comforting for almost 100 years.

This is the story of Crown Candy Kitchen. It is more than a collection of facts and photos, more than the story of one family. More, even, than just ice cream, candy, sandwiches and soups. Crown Candy Kitchen is a place where marriages have begun and where political deals have been fomented; where everyone from Babe Ruth to Carol Channing, and from the neighbor next door to the guy from Ladue have come for comfort, stability, and a certainty about "something" that was no longer present in their ever-changing lives. I hope you feel the spirits of the past — maybe even your own family's — as you read the story of ONE PLACE. ♛

Sweetness Preserved: THE STORY OF THE CROWN CANDY KITCHEN

The Beginnings

In any description of American History or the American Character, there are many themes that describe the experience of building the American nation. Perhaps no two are mentioned more as "the" definition of the American way than the "American Dream" and the "Melting Pot." The former has achieved iconic status in our folklore. Briefly, it means that the "land of opportunity" is available to anyone in America who is willing to sacrifice his or her time, talent and treasures to fulfill a dream. In short, anyone can be anything they wish to be in America, and the fulfillment of that ambition can be seen tangibly in conspicuous consumption: a home, a family, perhaps a car, and other belongings that signify "arrival." And it continues in the belief that each generation should/must achieve more than the previous one. A father's pride is seeing his son, and even his grandson, succeed more than he did.

In the metaphor of the "Melting Pot," there is arrival of another kind. From countries all over the world, more than 17 million people came through Ellis Island alone in the 50 years of its open doors. Fleeing persecution — religious, economic, social — or following the opportunities learned about in the oral tradition that found its way back to their countries: the belief that America was the land that welcomed everyone and encouraged them to seek their fortunes, and dared them to dream their dreams. In their accomplishments, the immigrants "melted" into a new land and a new beginning. Nationalities who at one time lived their lives intentionally segregated with their "own kind" now coexisted in neighborhoods that, on the one hand,

The early years in the store (far left), with the first salesmen.

Harry Karandzieff and his son, George (left) in the early days of the learning process.

Sweetness Preserved: THE STORY OF THE CROWN CANDY KITCHEN

Harry Karandzieff, the patriarch, the founder, the extraordinary candy man.

maintained their traditions and, on the other, tempered their mores to form an America where they, too, could pursue the "dream."

Harry Karandzieff, an immigrant from Macedonia, was a microcosm of these two American themes. One of seven children of Stanko and Christina Karandja living in a small village of Yugoslavian Macedonia, Harry, nicknamed "Decho," wanted to follow his brother Neumo to America to pursue his dream of running his own business and then helping his parents and siblings to have a better life in Greek-influenced Macedonia. In 1911, Harry made the journey from his family village of Kristalopigi, in the homeland of Alexander the Great, and shared the experience of millions before him. At Ellis Island, his surname changed in typically quirky fashion: from Karandja to Karandzieff. His destination in the U.S. depended on the stories of other Macedonians who settled in America: find the "colony" where his European traditions were still practiced within the American lifestyle. Madison, Illinois was the Mecca. Look for a livelihood or business with familiarity: confectioneries, so expertly developed by Greek immigrants and their neighbors. Find a place near enough to his traditions and people but far enough to establish his own identity. The answer: St. Louis, Missouri, across the Mississippi from Madison, Illinois.

Harry Karandzieff found his place in 1913. In the Murphy-Blair District of St. Louis, now known as "Old North St. Louis," on the northwest corner of St. Louis Avenue and 14th Street, stood a building that had been, in turn, a feed store,

CHAPTER 1: *The Beginning*

which catered to the thriving community's work animals, a tailor shop, and finally a shoe store. Charles Schlueter had erected the building in 1880 as a store on the first level with dwellings above it. Alterations were made to the storefront in 1911. But soon his business needed to expand, so in 1913 the entire building was put up for sale. Harry Karandzieff seized the opportunity, and Crown Candy Kitchen was born.

When Harry started his confectionery, he became part of a flourishing business district in which a merchants' association already had been established. In fact, the area had developed into one of the most attractive shopping districts in St. Louis. Among other businesses, there was a dry goods store connected to a tailor's shop, which at the time employed 40 tailors; furniture stores, where the furniture actually was made by immigrant carpenters; a spaghetti and macaroni factory; a hardware store (still in operation); saloons; several confectioneries; shoe stores; a cooperage for the expanding brewery industry; and feed stores. And, importantly, the area was populated by many different immigrant groups, heavily dominated by the Germans but sprinkled with Irish, Italians, Polish, Croatians, Macedonians, Greeks, and even some French settlers.

Into this thriving commerce, Harry brought his dream, and what he knew to be his destiny. He diligently sought out experts on the making of ice cream and candies. There were other confectioneries in the area that helped to train Harry in the business. He researched, participating and observing, and then applied what appealed to him. Inventing his own techniques, he slowly, even deliberately, fulfilled his dream: he became the "king" of St. Louis confectioners. Even synchronicity played a part.

Young George Karandzieff "taking five" during a rare break in the candy-making room.

Andy Karandzieff with Uncle Pete Jugaloff, the beginning of the education of a confectioner.

Harry needed a name for his new ice cream and candy store. One day, while cleaning out the wooden platform in the store window, he found a dirty, bent sign that was simply inscribed with the word CROWN. No need for further thought; he had found his name. But Harry wanted to make sure that everyone knew that his goods were handmade and that he created more than just candy and ice cream, so he added the "Kitchen." He believed that this would let people know that they could purchase sandwiches for lunches in addition to desserts. And to him, also, the word "kitchen" let people know that Crown was a place with a work ethic. All his life, Harry despised laziness. Grateful for the opportunity he had found in America, he wanted to be certain to publicize his belief in the need to apply oneself all the time.

Harry was so certain of the eventual success of his business, he dared to dream of a partner. And again, typical of the immigrant experience, just as he had been mentored in the ways of making candy and ice cream, he did the same for another immigrant who happened to be a relative. Pete Jugaloff, a Macedonian, was a second cousin to Harry's mother, Christina, and living in South St. Louis as a carpenter. When Harry asked him to join him in the business of confectionery, Pete locked into the same confidence and became a partner. With his carpentry skills and general handyman abilities, Pete became an invaluable member of the Crown Candy family. He built the wooden booths that are still used today in the very same configuration; he helped to design the candy cases and the soda fountain that also are still used today; he created the work surfaces for the candy making; and he was a troubleshooter for the ice cream machinery. He was "Uncle Pete" to all who knew him.

But there was one more part of the American Dream that Harry had yet to achieve: having a family to share

CHAPTER 1: *The Beginning*

CROWN
CANDY KITCHEN
GENEALOGY

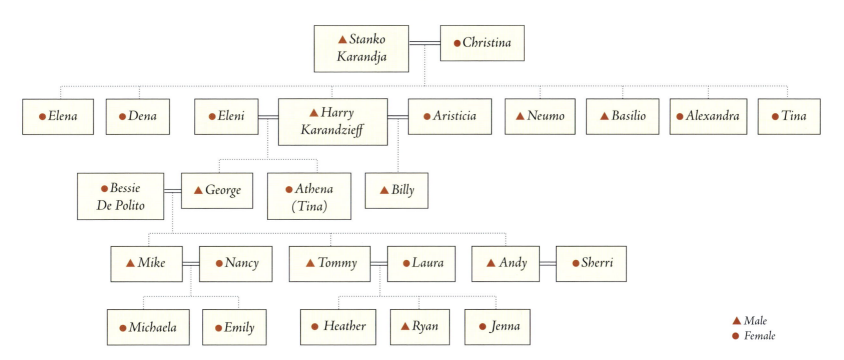

the dream and make it even bigger and better. It was at this time that Harry met Eleni, also an immigrant from Macedonia, who had come to America in another classic immigrant tradition: arranged marriages. Eleni (called Helen in America) was to be married to a Macedonian immigrant already in the States. Before she arrived, her future husband had died, and she was in America with no imminent marriage or chance to experience "the Dream." Enter Harry and listen for the wedding bells. All the parts of "opportunity" were now in place.

HOME MADE
Ice Cream
Special 25c Quart
BRICK OR LOOSE
with Flavor

CROWN CANDY KITCHEN

1401 ST. LOUIS AVE.
GARFIELD 9463

Harry and Eleni had two children, Athena and George. But as so often happens in the American epic, when George was 13 months old and Athena (called Tina) was three, Eleni died from what in those days was called "consumption" (tuberculosis). Harry was left a widower with a new business and a dream not yet accomplished.

But, interestingly, the pattern of the immigrant story continued. Harry had heard through the community about a Macedonian widow living in Chicago; he was encouraged to visit to determine a match for marriage. He followed his friends' advice and went to Chicago with his brother, Neumo, to meet her. In today's vernacular,

CHAPTER 1: *The Beginning*

Try Our Double Malted Milk 15¢

ICE CREAM SUNDAES

Cherry	10c	Orange	10c	Pineapple	10c
Vanilla	10c	Chocolate	10c	Lemon	10c
Strawberry	10c	Caramel	10c	Banana	10c
		Marshmallow	10c	Maple	10c

SODAS

Crushed Fruit Sodas—Pineapple, Cherry or Strawberry . . . 15c

Vanilla	10c	Strawberry	10c	Maple	10c
Cherry	10c	Orange	10c	Coca-Cola	
Chocolate	10c	Banana	10c	Sodas	15c
Root Beer	10c	Pineapple	10c		

Served with Whipped Cream 5c extra

SPECIALS

Butter-Pecan	15c	Pineapple Pecan	15c
Swiss Chocolate	15c	Nut Sundae	15c
Nabisco	15c	Fruit Salad	15c
Cherry Pecan	15c	Strawberry Pecan	15c

All Two-Flavor Sundaes 15c
Sundaes with Whipped Cream 15c

SANDWICHES

Roast Pork	10c	Cheese	10c
Roast Beef	10c	Melted Cheese on Toast	15c
Baked Ham	10c	Bacon Lettuce	10c
Fried Ham on Toast	15c	Bacon, Lettuce and Tomato	15c
Egg Salad	10c	Ham and Egg	15c
Ham Salad	10c	Bacon and Egg	15c
Cube Steak	10c	Hamburger	10c
Pork Chops	10c	Combination	15c
Salmon Salad	10c		

Lettuce and Tomato on Sandwiches 5c extra

All Pie, per Cut . . 10c   A la Mode . . . 15c

NEWPORTS

Served with Whipped Cream and Nuts

Cherry	20c	Strawberry	20c
Chocolate	20c	Pineapple	20c

SPECIAL SUNDAES

Banana Split	20c	French Sundae	25c
Club House Nut	25c	Lovers Delight	25c
Fresh Banana Sundae	15c	Uncle Sam	25c
Double Frozen Malted Milk—All Flavors as Sundaes			15c
Caramel, Root-Beer or Coca-Cola Malted Milk			20c
Milk Shake			15c
All Phosphates			5 and 10c
Bulk or Brick Ice Cream . . . Quart 25c . . . Pint			15c

PLATE LUNCH

Soup	10c	Small Steak	30c
Roast Pork	30c	Pork Chop	30c
Roast Beef	30c	Ham and Egg	30c
Salmon Salad	30c	Bacon and Egg	30c
Vegetable Dinner	30c	Chili Mac	15c
Cold Ham	30c	Chili	10c
Hamburger Steak	30c		

Coffee, Milk, Soda Extra with Dinners 5c
Hot Chocolate . . 10c   With Whipped Cream . . 15c

— SPECIALS —

An early menu from Crown Candy Kitchen, featuring their extra-thick chocolate malt for only 15 cents.

there was no "connection;" but, as it happened, Harry met another Macedonian widow, Aristicia, and found an ideal match. Aristicia had a house and property; she sold both and put the proceeds into the business in St. Louis. Together, she and Harry had one son, William, who was born with cerebral palsy. What might have been a nightmare to others with the American Dream did not put off Harry. With the same determination he showed in his resolve to establish a successful business, Harry and his wife accepted their fate, and Billy, too, became an integral member of the confectionery staff. In fact, George became so attached to his little brother that he helped to raise him, mentored him in the business to the best of Billy's abilities, and supported him after his parents died.

So the opening act of Crown Candy Kitchen was set. Harry, Aristicia, Uncle Pete and the kids, George and Tina, developed the business plan that is still operative today. It was time now to develop the brand that would become world famous! ♛

Sweetness Preserved: THE STORY OF THE CROWN CANDY KITCHEN

Developing a Brand

Working with the creeds, "know your place in the world" and "treat your customers as family," the owners of Crown Candy Kitchen began their enterprise. They knew that they wanted to be in the confectionery business, to make the best handmade candy and ice cream, and to settle into that vision as their little corner of the world. They believed that if they did a good job of producing quality products, they would succeed. Their "place" in the world was at the northwest corner of St. Louis Avenue and 14th Street.

They believed also that the business would grow if people became part of their extended family. Customers were their lifeblood and should be greeted as family, treated as guests, and served the highest-quality products.

In the beginning, Harry, Pete and Eleni made only three flavors of ice cream: vanilla, chocolate, and strawberry, using 300 pounds of ice and rock salt daily and the exhausting hand-crank method of manufacture. In the beginning, ice cream cones, with two dips, sold for five cents; sundaes with chocolate syrup sold for 10 cents. Eventually, they added chocolate ice cream sodas using carbonated water, phosphates in six different flavors, and their signature malt.

The back room was used for candy making. German candy makers had come to St. Louis to ply their trade and, as with the manufacture of ice cream, Harry and Pete were invited to watch these masters make their candy. Eventually, their observation as apprentices taught them how to develop the product that became Crown candy. From those same German confectioners, the Karandzieffs purchased candy molds for Easter

The soda fountain (far left), where for more than 90 years people have been served the special ice cream creations.

Crown Candy Kitchen (left), just opening up for another busy day.

Sweetness Preserved: THE STORY OF THE CROWN CANDY KITCHEN

Andy prepares the icy cold malts while Denice delivers water to the tables.

bunnies and for "St. Nikolas." There were tin molds in various sizes — bunnies as tall as 24 inches and as heavy as five pounds, for example, were part of the production of chocolates at Easter.

In time, the "customer family" wanted more. Harry and Pete always knew that desserts and candy were not enough fare. They added "plate" lunches so that a complete meal, crowned by the ice cream and candy desserts, could be served. In the thriving neighborhood and business district, Harry's philosophy to "grow" his family was increasingly successful. In time, other confectioneries in the neighborhood closed; some became saloons, while others became shoe stores or dry goods stores. The service orientation of Crown Candy Kitchen and the care that the Karandzieffs put into their products and company philosophy were reaping enormous benefits. Their dedication to quality kept them thriving and outlasting other confectioneries.

The family, including Uncle Pete, occupied the apartment dwellings above the store. The convenience of these living quarters had become a necessity in 16-hour workdays, seven days a week, that were required to achieve the American Dream. But they knew they had found their niche.

Also during this time, they were developing more signature products, like Heavenly Hash. Marshmallows, hand dipped in chocolate and covered with fresh, chocolate-covered, butter-roasted pecans became an instant best seller and have remained so for 85 years. In addition, Harry and Pete's relationship with Coca-Cola as the "pop" of choice eventually led to a hobby-business of collecting Coca-Cola advertising products, especially the original trays, featuring Gibson Girls enjoying a sip of the cool beverage. Signs, posters, cups, glasses, commemorative bottles of Coca-Cola — all became identified with Crown Candy and were used as museum-

CHAPTER 2: *Developing a Brand*

like decorations around the walls. They allowed for a familiarity, a slice of Americana, an invitation to enjoy the moment as regular as a visit to a favorite grandmother's home.

Harry's vision was expanding. The work was tiring, requiring 100 per cent commitment from both Harry and Pete. But they never wavered, and they created a solid foundation for the confectionery that outlasted all of them, not only in the 14th Street business district, but throughout St. Louis in the first three decades of the 20th century.

There was never any question about their children, George and Tina, working in the restaurant. They were groomed almost from birth, steeped in a strong work ethic and the motto of their father. Eventually, Tina took over the kitchen and developed the lunches and suppers that are still served today. Not only did she prepare pork, beef, or ham dinners, but she also developed sandwiches, which could be eaten more quickly and still leave enough room for the ice cream desserts. The Bacon-Lettuce-Tomato — BLT— became THE Crown sandwich, with its dozen strips of bacon and fresh tomatoes serving as comfort food for customers experiencing personal and national traumas.

The making of candy and ice cream specialties was still the job of Harry and Pete. And George became a willing and eager student of the business. At age seven, he set up a popcorn stand just outside the store, setting his own price at five cents a bag. His natural bent for merchandising and customer service was developing before his teens. But it was the making of candy and ice cream that represented the creative act, selfless sharing, and a deep desire to make people happy that primarily appealed to George. From the time he was able to walk, he was aware of the production of both candy and ice cream "in his home." Hanging around the candy-making area, watching intently, sampling frequently, asking little, George learned the art of the confectioner from his idealistic father and workaholic uncle. And he, himself, became a perfectionist and driven professional in the art of confectionery. George symbolized the future for Crown Candy Kitchen.

A small part of the Coca-Cola memorabilia that distinguishes Crown Candy Kitchen.

The 90-year-old glass cabinet, with its ornate art glass, stands in the corner of the soda fountain.

An early promotional thermometer from Baden Ice Cream Co. next to an early Coke print that lines the walls.

In fact, it was George, developing the candy specialties — "Snappers," nut clusters, molasses puffs, and countless other designs — who became the biggest factor in the early successes of the business. His effervescent personality was natural, contagious and wondrously appealing. To him, Crown Candy was not a place simply to buy food or candy or ice cream, but a place where each sale evoked a smile; where each person forgot his troubles; where everyone left in a better mood than when they came in. Seven days a week, even while he was attending school, George lived to make "his piece of pie" a place of joy, happiness, nostalgia, memories and meaning. It was his mission, and his medium was the candy and ice cream. They became, and still are, George's "real world theology." And, during caramel or pecan dips, he loved to emphasize his belief by shaking hands with customers with his chocolate-drenched fingers. For many people, licking the slightly warm chocolate from their fingers after George shook their hands became a favorite childhood memory.

But World War II intruded into George's world of "meaningful ice cream." He joined the Army in 1944, became a tank driver, and served overseas until 1946. This 20-year old continued the patriotic American

pattern followed by his father and uncle: America gave us freedom, so thanks were in order. But ice cream and candy were never far from his mind. He believed he would return to the States to continue the mission he had established: spread joy to everyone through his confections.

It was in 1946, when he returned to St. Louis, that George Karandzieff met Bessie De Polito. Bessie was a neighborhood resident who frequented Crown Candy Kitchen with her girlfriends. It was the typical gathering place for teenagers to "just hang" and learn to grow up.

CHAPTER 2: *Developing a Brand*

The girlfriends introduced Bessie to George, and in 1950 they were married at the Greek Orthodox Church in St. Louis. Another chapter in the history of Crown Candy Kitchen was about to begin.

Having served his country for two years and having worked at Crown for some two decades, George was ready to take over the business. Following the dream of his immigrant father, George continued the tradition of confectionery. Harry continued to make the ice cream and candy, and Pete, also, served, as the congenial jack-of-all-trades. But both of them knew that it was time to pass the baton, and George Karandzieff, newly married, eagerly accepted it. The second generation — in the same place, with the same ethic, the same professionalism, the same quality product — became worthy successors.

So, in 30 short years, a "brand" unique to St. Louis had been established in the North Side. The reputation of Crown's superior and delicious homemade ice cream and chocolate candy specialties had grown citywide. The tiny dream had become a tradition unique in its consistency, quality and stability. Everyone who entered Crown Candy Kitchen knew that they could get the same delicious ice cream and the same creamy chocolates no matter what time of the day or year they visited. It became one constant in the fast-developing world that had changed so quickly through two world wars. Many a St. Louisan took comfort in their visits to Crown Candy. In fact, by the end of the '40s, one only had to mention Crown, and everyone freely associated the name with ice cream and candy. It was left only for the nation to experience the brand. ♛

Ready for Valentine's Day with eight pounds of chocolates in the center box.

St. Nicholas (above) from the old German molds. Five pounds of pleasure!

Sweetness Preserved: THE STORY OF THE CROWN CANDY KITCHEN

The Tradition Must Continue

Harry was still managing the business when his son, George, returned from serving in the Army. Uncle Pete was still the ideal jack-of-all-trades and the "rock" for the Karandzieff family. But both Harry and Pete knew that the long hours necessary to keep the business successful were getting longer and they were getting older. Enter the American pattern of the son becoming the "father" and taking over a business.

After the war, George became the real force behind the operations of Crown Candy Kitchen. Eventually, his sister, Tina, retired to raise a family. And although his father, Harry, and his Uncle Pete were still working at the store, George became the vision. He had the business sense and the personality to make certain that the consistency of Crown Candy would continue.

Fresh from a war and filled with a new purpose, George devoted all his waking hours to running the confectionery. Bessie, his wife, took a job at Woolworth's to ensure that there would be a steady weekly paycheck, but she also worked evenings and Sundays at Crown, packing candy. She enthusiastically shared her husband's vision for the business.

With Harry and Pete getting older, George always hoped that he, too, would have a son to continue the business and the American "pattern." Heaven smiled on him and Bessie: as he often says, he "was blessed with not one, but three sons," who bought into his vision and his work ethic.

Enter Michael Ricky (1954), Thomas Angelo (1956), and Andrew Norman (1964). There was never any demand that these three sons would follow in their

Mike Karandzieff (far left) preparing for the daily rush of customers and wondering how many malts he'll make.

Homemade chocolate sauce (at left), made weekly, simmering in the antique copper pot and severely tempting chocoholics.

Sweetness Preserved: THE STORY OF THE CROWN CANDY KITCHEN

George Karandzieff with his perpetual smile, even though he had worked through the night making candies.

father's footsteps, but George hoped that one or two or, ideally, all three see the enjoyment of the candy and ice cream business and share in his dreams.

Mike, the oldest, was born upstairs in the family living quarters over the store. When he was 10 years old, he worked weekends in the store washing dishes and sanitizing the equipment. But he also learned the important craft of making ice cream and creating ice cream specialties during his apprentice years. Mentored by his father, Mike's art became second nature.

Most importantly, however, Mike learned customer relations from observing a "natural" teacher, his father, George. But when the time came to make a decision on a career, whether to join the business or not, Mike decided college was the proper route. He had worked at Crown for nine years and he wanted to experience some alternatives to a soda fountain. So for two years he pursued collegiate studies, and even worked delivering furniture. No one questioned his decision, but wisely encouraged him to do what he felt he had to do. Grandfather Harry, Uncle Pete and his father, George, continued to work the store and seemed to be "holding on." But soon, the assurance of a job at Crown, with a steady paycheck and a known product, appealed to Mike more than finishing college and pushing furniture. With the blessings of his father and uncle — and to their great relief — he became a regular at the soda fountain. Eventually, Mike took over making all the ice cream and served as the soda jerk, creating specialties and happily waiting on customers. Mike also made certain that the candy counter in the front of the store was always filled and presentable. (He still does.) And at Easter and Christmas, when candy sales are especially brisk, Mike arranges for more tables to display the chocolate figures, establishes a system of ordering the candy, and makes certain that everyone has the proper, legendary and memorable customer experience.

Today, with knees painful from nearly four decades of standing and working 15-hour days, Mike still makes almost all the ice cream and still supervises all the candy displays. The chocolate Santas standing regally in rows

CHAPTER 3: *The Tradition Must Continue*

at Christmastime; the solid chocolate rabbits at Easter, in dozens of different shapes; the inviting chocolate hearts on Valentine's Day, evoking the innocence of a first love — all are the work of Mike Karandzieff.

Gruffly perfectionistic, Mike requires and teaches the vision of his ancestors: always evoke nostalgia for a carefree time that must not be forgotten. Ask about the history of a candy mold, or a new chocolate presentation, or the art of the chocolatier, and Mike will educate you. His displays reflect a time of childhood innocence that he believes should never be lost. Candy, to him, is history, a past of pleasant memories. Keep the giant jawbreakers and the rock candy and the licorice whips! They serve as a link to Mike's past, and his style almost demands that they be presented consistently and correctly. To him they represent the never-changing ethic of Crown Candy Kitchen. He is the archivist who, through candy, preserves for generations. For Mike, this job is more than a college education; he has lived it. And his wife, Nancy, and his two young daughters, Michaela and Emily, enthusiastically support the "museum" that is Crown Candy.

Tommy, too, the second son of Bessie and George, and also born upstairs from the store, worked at Crown from the time he was 10 years old. When he started, he did the same kind of work his brother and father had done when they began: emptying trash, washing dishes, and general cleanup. But instead of making the candy and the ice cream (Mike did teach him the methods of doing the latter), Tommy was educated in another facet of the family business by his aunt, Tina — the all-important kitchen. He learned the art of preparing food, keeping it warm and serving it on time, and keeping the kitchen sparkling. Eventually, after Tina retired, Tommy became the head chef and ran the kitchen. He perfected the BLT and the Reuben — the two biggest sellers — and added a new chili recipe, soups, chicken salad, egg salad, and some specials like a turkey melt and Crown salads. In the tradition of multi-tasking started by his father and grandfather, Tommy works on weekends as the soda jerk. He wants to make sure that he hasn't abandoned his craft completely.

Andy, Bessie, Mike, and Tommy Karandzieff (left to right) right after the boys took over the business.

Sweetness Preserved: THE STORY OF THE CROWN CANDY KITCHEN

George Karandzieff doing what he loves the most: talking with kids and showing them how the soda fountain works.

Importantly, Tommy serves as the very outgoing greeter for all deliveries. His mornings are spent "goofing" on long-time delivery men, asking about their families, and giving his opinion on current affairs, sports — whatever. Tommy doesn't know a stranger, and his even temper and non-stop chatter cooly reflect the store's ambiance.

Tommy's natural warmth even extends to the cats in the neighborhood. Sometimes called the "St. Francis of St. Louis Avenue," Tommy makes certain that "his" cats are promptly and regularly fed at the back door each morning. The scene is right out of an early movie newsreel of immigrant life on the lower East Side. This morning ritual unconsciously reflects the nurturing qualities of the Karandzieff vision.

Tommy is also supported by his wife, Laura, and their three children: Heather, Ryan and Jenna. All of the kids have worked in the store doing various tasks at one time or another, and Ryan has even learned to make ice cream, which he does frequently. The beat goes on!

The third son, and last child of George and Bessie, Andy, was not born above the store. The family had moved to a larger home in North St. Louis County to accommodate their growing family. It was here that Andy arrived, breaking the pattern of the "stage-door" birth. But he, too, worked the soda fountain, learning from the ground up, as his brothers had done. Being the youngest, however, Andy did not have the same expectations as his brothers. After high school, he decided to attend a junior college; but, having trouble deciding on a major, becoming more aware of his temperament and knowing his abilities, he decided to follow his grandfather, father, uncle and brothers

CHAPTER 3: *The Tradition Must Continue*

in the soda fountain and candy business. Andy is a natural for the job — perhaps even the most suited, with his personality, of all the generations of Karandzieffs to have toiled at Crown Candy.

Uncle Pete and Andy had a special relationship, a bond different from any others. It was Pete who mentored the teenager Andy in the business and taught him the importance of learning all aspects of the store. Ice cream making, the art of chocolate, the process of preparing molds, curing the chocolate, creating its presentation, "cleaning" the product, even the shine of the chocolate — all of this, Andy picked up from Uncle Pete and his father, George. This pride in craft and workmanship, instilled by Uncle Pete, serves as Andy's singular motivation. He has become the master chocolatier who carefully, diligently and proudly pours all the molds for holiday chocolates. Like his brothers in their specialties, Andy is eager to maintain a consistent product and a Crown Candy tradition. Eight tons of chocolate are melted annually to serve the increasing clientele; but to Andy, individual, conscientious care to each molded product is still required. The hours in production are longer, but the chocolates produced are the same quality product that Crown Candy Kitchen has turned out for more than 90 years.

The packing room at Crown Candy, where more of the Coca-Cola memorabilia is displayed.

Andy sees himself, more than anyone, as the "keeper of the recipe, and the preserver of the past" — and always a chocolate historian, because "it is necessary to maintain what is good."

But making chocolate creations is not Andy's only role in the business. When he is out in front making the ice cream desserts, his creative, endless bantering with customers — policemen, lawyers, judges, firefighters and regulars — adds a critical element of "Cheers" to the

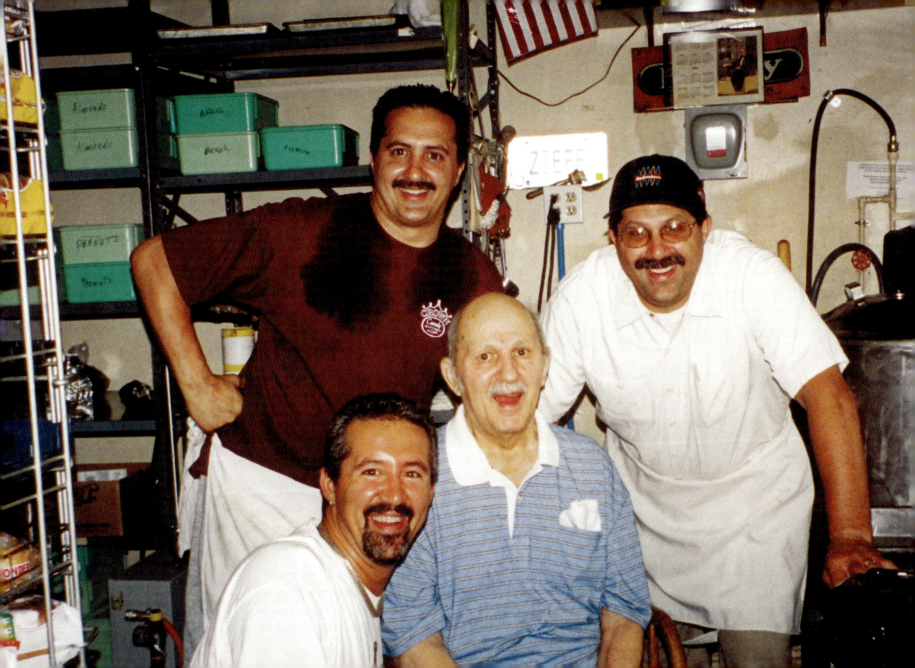

CHAPTER 3: The Tradition Must Continue

business. This remarkable awareness of people that Andy possesses — remembering names, their regular orders, some connection to their families, their politics or favorite sports, their occupations — eerily echoes the personalities of his grandfather, Harry, and his Uncle Pete.

Andy also is the ombudsman for Crown Candy. From serving as a one-man public relations department for the store, to mediating workers' conflicts, overseeing accounts, developing the brand further, making all the candy and managing its shipping and packing, performing all jobs required of the soda jerk, and, finally, to providing very personal customer service, Andy does it.

Andy and his wife, Sherri, live above the store in the apartment formerly occupied by so many Karandzieffs. And up there, living in the apartment, the family now has come full circle.

In 1991, Mike, Tommy and Andy, following the American tradition, took over the ownership of Crown Candy Kitchen from their father. George, who had always secretly hoped that his sons would keep it going, felt confident in the continued success of the business.

Harry Karandzieff, the founder of Crown Candy, died in 1965; Uncle Pete Jugaloff died in 1984 at age 94. Pete had refused to retire and always found some little task to be completed at Crown. He was active in his "real love" for the store, working fewer hours but dedicated until the very end. George decided to retire from a fulltime job at Crown Candy at age 75, but he still makes weekly visits to the establishment to observe his masterpiece.

So now it is the business of the boys, who have taken the history of Crown Candy Kitchen from 1913 and keep it magical. Steady, business-like, Mike; the even-tempered Tommy; and the extroverted optimist, Andy, complement each other very well. They have taken the lessons from their master teachers and made them their own, but they have not sacrificed their historically high standards of consistency, tradition, quality or customer service.

All three of them know that this place is special, and they are determined to keep it so. It's not about the candy, or the molds, or the ice cream individually; it's about the total package that they represent. Their place is a museum to be experienced, not quietly or reverently, but with a contagious joyfulness that reminds us what goodness, simplicity and consistency are. ♛

George with his sons, Andy, Tommy, and Mike near the chocolate melting tubs, enjoying another successful Easter season.

Sweetness Preserved: THE STORY OF THE CROWN CANDY KITCHEN

The Supporting Cast

Harry, Pete, George, Mike, Tommy and Andy have always managed Crown Candy Kitchen hands-on, conscientiously and willingly. Over the years, one, two, or — most of the time, all of them, in any generation — have been at the establishment at the same time. Again, it was their dream, their commitment and their job to make sure that the magic of Crown Candy Kitchen would always be consistent and present.

However, because of the success of the place over nine decades, they needed a crew of like-minded individuals who could support the dream. Besides the part-time help of the wives, the Karandzieffs typically hired neighborhood residents to help manage during all hours of operations.

Dishwashing, waitressing, maintaining equipment and providing custodial help, working in the kitchen, packing candy, helping at the counter and various other jobs obviously had to be done. Amazingly, the neighborhood hires had, by some magic of "contagion," in a manner never stated but demonstrated, shared the mission and vision of Crown Candy Kitchen. There was never a need to advertise for help; neighbors became the employees and played a critical role in the success of Crown Candy.

Throughout the years, of the many waitresses, three are especially tied to the history of Crown Candy. Bonnie Brogan and the twins, Tammy Siebels and Pam Mardirosian (née Goebel), have so understood what the meaning of Crown Candy Kitchen was to the St. Louis area that they often have been taken for family. Bonnie worked for more than 40 years before her untimely death from cancer, and

Pam Mardirosian, one of the twin waitresses, proudly wearing her shirt of triumph over the 1983 fire.

Tammy Siebels and Bonnie Brogan await the busy lunch crowd.

John Magee dips strawberries into the milky chocolate and Tom Burgoon packs them for Valentine's Day.

Tammy and her twin, Pam, prepare for the day with Tommy.

Tammy and Pam each have worked at Crown for more than 27 years. Their tenures are far longer than those of any other employees.

Not only did these three ladies wait tables, but they also dipped chocolates, made sandwiches, ran the cash register and monitored the candy counter. And their hours often were as long as those of the Karandzieff family members. Each of them, with their unique personalities, contributed to the lore of Crown Candy Kitchen.

Bonnie was so involved during many hours of the business that George referred to her as his "adopted daughter." She helped celebrate family events, took part in their rites of passage, and even took care of unmarried and ailing Uncle Pete during his last 10 years. And Bonnie, like Pam and Tammy, knew everyone who came into the store on a regular basis. She was a careful student of human nature who knew when to be appropriately sassy, comforting, quiet or joking. She kept track of customers' families and friends, served as the news conduit, and never wrote down any order. Throughout her conversations, she never forgot what the customer ordered. Dutifully, but appropriately, she screamed her order to whoever was making the ice cream creations. Bonnie was one of a kind, who never knew any enemy and was a perfect fit with the tradition of the founders as far back as Harry. When she died in 2003, Crown Candy Kitchen closed its doors in her honor.

The twins, Tammy and Pam, also lived in the neighborhood around Crown Candy. They were the

CHAPTER 4: The Supporting Cast

seventh and eighth children of the Goebel family, which had frequented Crown on a regular basis. Outgoing and unassuming, with an outstanding work ethic and knowledge of the neighborhood, they were a perfect fit with the Karandzieffs' goals.

Tammy, the self-described "talkative" one, became the quintessential waitress. She, too, never writes down an order, almost never makes a mistake, and also greets her customers most often by name. If she doesn't know someone's name when they come into Crown Candy, she knows it by the time they leave. Her joking and jovial manner; her optimistic outlook; her genuine love of people — all have been strong contributions to the continuing success of Crown Candy. And, of course, like the owners, when not busy as a waitress, Tammy packs candy or even dips strawberries in the rich, creamy chocolate during their season.

Pam, the 15-minute-younger twin, serves as the main cashier and "general" of take-out orders. She prefers monetary transactions to the waitress gig. But she also is adept at making lunches, the famous Heavenly Hash — usually 50 pounds at a time — and pronounces herself the "official bouncer." Known for her snappy comebacks and hearty laugh, Pam gets to greet each customer as they enter and leave. There are friendly gags of many years' running with some customers; there are concerned questions about family members; and there is sometimes just the "stare" when someone wants to know if the banana malt tastes like a banana.

Tammy and Pam, Pam and Tammy — mistaken for each other wherever they might go. But they have distinct personalities, and they are separate, contributing members of the Crown Candy legacy.

In the early days, the waitresses had a "not very favorite uniform look."

Jerry greeting customers from his position behind the fountain, preparing the bowls for the sundaes.

Sweetness Preserved: THE STORY OF THE CROWN CANDY KITCHEN

Preparing take-out sandwiches in the early days. (above)

Rose Sadowski (right) hand-dipping the large strawberries for Mother's Day.

Denice Chaffin is another important member of the wait staff at Crown. She served as a "weekend warrior" for 15 years but, when Bonnie died, Denice became the regular weekday waitress and fell into the same appealing pattern. Quiet and dedicated, Denice fits the desired work ethic of the whole crew. And she, too, packs chocolates in the various-sized boxes when there is the infrequent lull in the store. Denice also was a neighborhood kid, so she understands the philosophy and history of the business. And, like Tammy and Bonnie before her, Denice needs no order forms either.

From the time that Harry and Pete founded the store, the Karandzieffs have had an important operating philosophy about people that today would be labeled "multiculturalism." Recognizing their roots and the manner in which they were accepted into the American mainstream, for 90 years they have instilled in all members of their family who have managed the business the importance of valuing diversity, accepting people for their own uniqueness, and allowing

someone to grow through their guidance and business product. The rest of the employees who work at Crown Candy are an admirable mix of diversity that works because of the respect engendered by the Karandzieffs.

For example, they have hired home-schooled brothers who live in the neighborhood and have trained them to work the front counter and prep the take-out lunches; twin sisters, also from the neighborhood, to work as waitresses on the weekends; two men to serve as *sous* chefs and dishwashers, by turn, who happen to be African American and hearing impaired; several down-on-their-luck men who need employment to restore not only their funds but also their dignity; and a few teenaged neighborhood kids who need "real-world" experience in business. Their proximity to the establishment allows Crown to use them on as-needed basis, in addition to their scheduled working hours.

CHAPTER 4: *The Supporting Cast*

None of these employees was hired by happenstance. They had to have a work ethic, to be sure, but their diversity continues to reflect the philosophy of the Karandzieffs. As immigrants from Macedonia, they were given a chance to realize the American dream, and they succeeded. The family believes that others who may need a helping hand should have the same chance to succeed. Not only has Crown Candy Kitchen developed a landmark tradition with this philosophy, but it also has been enormously influential in maintaining the neighborhood's ethnic diversity and has been a catalyst for hundreds of new homes being built in the area.

In a very real sense, the tradition of Crown Candy Kitchen is deeper and more significant than the candy and ice cream they make and sell. People, no matter their race or orientation, can make a difference if they are treated with respect, managed honestly and encouraged to learn by mistakes. The Karandzieff family was way ahead of their culture. From the beginning, they have thumbed their noses at cultural collisions. People are people; it's that simple. So Crown Candy creates opportunities for success, values differences in people, and educates others by example.

There is no written strategic plan, nor any business plan to be tweaked every year. And even though the owners say that Crown Candy works in spite of itself, there is, in their spirit, mind, and "gut" The Plan, which is in one sense old-fashioned, but in another sense *avant garde*.

The family is not all related by blood, but by the universal themes that Crown Candy represents, as summed up in the "Platinum Rule" — treat others as they would like to be treated. And, by the way, they produce a superior product! ♛

Too busy to talk, a uniformed waitress is rushing to get a luncheon order.

Nicki Boatright (center) greets the first customer of the day on her Saturday shift.

The Folklore of the Crown Candy Kitchen

When an establishment like Crown Candy survives for 90 years selling ice cream made with the same recipe, and candy, using the same molds, and serving the same customers and their families day after day, there is certain to be an oral tradition surrounding the activities. People's experiences while dining at the confectionary are tempered by a nostalgia that becomes greater and more comforting with each visit. And the lore continues to develop and grow and becomes the tradition of Crown Candy Kitchen. Consider the following.

"Jeopardy!"

In 2002, there was a question about Crown Candy Kitchen on the nationally syndicated television game show, "Jeopardy!" Before millions of viewers, contestants were expected to know a piece of trivia about a soda fountain in St. Louis. This expectation underscores the attraction of a local confectionery on a national level.

The answer: "Crown Candy Kitchen, in St. Louis, is famous for this contest."

The question: "What is: if you can eat/drink five malts within a half-hour you get them free of charge?" And a contestant got it right!

It is difficult to exaggerate the significance of this question on a national game show. The fame of Crown Candy Kitchen had reached a level of consequence so large that the shop was no longer just a soda fountain but an attraction. It was an historically significant occasion. The names of the customers who have consumed five malts within 30 minutes are inscribed on a plaque in Crown Candy. Here, then, are the 15 champions, in the manner

The Easter Monkey prepares for his role in the Easter celebration and wonders if he'll be caught.

The "plaque of honor" lists those brave malt lovers who consumed 5 of them within 30 minutes.

This malt is only one of the 2-and-a-half glasses of the entire 24-ounce malt! Can you drink five malts in less than a half an hour?

and order in which they are inscribed:

1. Steve "Conan" Frein: 9/91 (no time listed)

2. Mark Matthew Vondras: 15 minutes

3. Patrick O'Brien: 19 minutes

4. James Moeller: 30 minutes; 1999

5. Patrick O'Brien: 18 minutes, 54 seconds (a two-time champion); 11/21/93

6. Bill Litteken: 27 minutes; 8/01/95

7. Pastor Ron Rall: 29 minutes, 55 seconds

8. Doug Reynolds: 18 minutes; 7/25/97

9. Francet Lee: 25 minutes (the first woman on the list); 6/08/02

10. John George Frangoulis: February 24, 1995 (no time listed)

11. Jim Corner: 29 minutes, 45 seconds

12. Warren Doherty: 20 minutes

13. Mike Martinez: 29 minutes, 55 seconds

14. Robert Steffan: 29 minutes, 25 seconds

15. Grand champion (so far): Richard Lefevre, 25 minutes. 6 Malts

The Ghost of Uncle Pete

Uncle Pete Jugaloff, who had become the jack-of-all-trades at Crown Candy Kitchen after he joined the business as a carpenter, was 5'10" tall, stocky, muscular, and self-described as "strong as an ox." He did not have the personality or disposition of his cousin, Harry, but his work ethic was unparalleled. There were seasons when he simply worked all day getting the chocolates made or the ice cream completed, or making repairs on the equipment. In fact, Pete was THE expert in making taffy and fudge. Eventually, he taught Mike to make those candies, but Pete always believed that no one did it as well as he.

Pete was a quiet man who lived upstairs from the store in one of the apartments Harry had remodeled.

CHAPTER 5: *The Folklore of the Crown Candy Kitchen*

But his quiet demeanor deceptively allowed for no nonsense by the customers. For example, described by some as silent as Harpo Marx, Uncle Pete, while working the fountain, would gaze at a teenage customer who was acting up and point his finger at the door, and the teenager would leave. There was no need to argue or complain; Uncle Pete had had enough and nothing would change his mind. Pete used the same stare with the employees when they were "relaxing" too much. Everyone knew the meaning of THE STARE.

When he did allow himself some free time, he loved the racetrack on the East Side and had friends take him there, since he did not drive. Pete would take only so much money — $20— and it had to be exactly that amount every time — and when it was gone, he left the track.

Pete also identified people with his own quirky nicknames. Mike was "Rabbi Mike" and Tommy was "Banana Peddler Tommy." No one knew the origins of these names, but they stuck with some people, and Uncle Pete relished the laughter associated with them. His sense of humor was pointed, inoffensive and likeable.

Andy, the youngest of the brothers, was especially close to Uncle Pete. Often, Pete would tease Andy by hiding money under the counters and then telling Andy that it was time to sweep up. Young Andy would find money everywhere and was excited about this new-found wealth. Pete enjoyed the charade. He took a special liking to Andy, and it was Pete who mentored Andy in many of the crafts and duties of the store.

Pete's stamina and strength was so great that he worked well into his 80s, doing everything he did when

The crates made by Uncle Pete Jugaloff many decades ago that hold all the old candy molds used for the holidays.

Sweetness Preserved: THE STORY OF THE CROWN CANDY KITCHEN

Andy prepares milk chocolate to be given as Christmas cards that you can eat!

he was younger, but at a slower pace. He even repaired the roof, by himself, when he was 85 years old! Climbing the long extension ladders was a small feat to this "old, strong ox."

But, in his 80s, Pete did take some time to watch TV during his daily breaks, which he never took when he was younger. He placed a television in the back room next to the kitchen, bought a rocking chair and religiously watched his favorite program, "Sanford and Son," starring Redd Foxx. He could even tell you some of the dialogue while watching repeats and often pointed to Sanford's activities while laughing hilariously. Watching TV, he always had his staples nearby: whiskey and apples! Sometimes he also ate the hot peppers that he had grown in his backyard garden.

In the vernacular, Pete was a "character" who helped to create legends about himself; and, when the subject was Pete, the material was exhaustive. For years after his death, his eccentricities were fodder for many stories.

He died at age 94 from cancer, which he had fought for some five years. But during that time, the racetrack kept calling as his only vice. The "ponies" were good medicine for him.

About two years after Pete's death, Andy was working one day in the kitchen area, and when he looked over to the next room, he saw a specter of a person in a rocking chair pointing to something on the table. He recognized the silhouette as Uncle Pete, sitting in his rocking chair, watching TV and pointing to Redd Foxx. Andy told no one of his vision. But about two weeks after he saw the specter, two of the waitresses swore that they saw a ghost who looked like Uncle Pete pointing at them from the door. His signature, pointed finger was seen in both instances. They were unafraid but told Andy about the sighting, and it confirmed for him what he also had seen.

Most recently, Denice Chaffin, one of the waitresses, saw a specter coming out of the ice cream manufacturing area. He was dressed in a white T-shirt with cigarettes rolled up in his short sleeve on top of his shoulder. Never having known Uncle Pete, Denice described the ghost to the Karandzieff family, and they were all certain that it was Pete.

CHAPTER 5: The Folklore of the Crown Candy Kitchen

According to Denice, Pete, "the ghost," proceeded to the back room, where he usually watched TV, and she did not see him again and has never seen him since.

There have been other indications of Uncle Pete's presence, also. In places where he used to hide coins for Andy to find, and that only Andy and Pete knew, coins have mysteriously appeared. On one occasion, laughter was heard in the room next to the kitchen where Pete had laughed very loudly as he watched TV. Three people heard it, but only one of them had known about Uncle Pete and related the story.

The ghost of Uncle Pete continues to be a legend at Crown Candy Kitchen. Those who were closest to him welcome his presence and treat it as good luck. Uncle Pete is still watching over the store.

The Easter Monkey

Tim Ezell, the endearingly wacky, unique, clever, daily "fun" reporter for KTVI-TV, Channel 2, the FOX affiliate in St. Louis, helped to create a folklore about Crown Candy that resulted in a chocolate specialty's becoming a best seller. During one of his daily, early morning reports, Ezell told this story of the Easter Monkey to all his listeners:

"Unlike Santa Claus, who has Dancer, Prancer, Vixen, Rudolph, and the gang, the Easter Bunny has to travel alone. So, the Easter Bunny was having a hard time getting to everyone since he had as much ground to cover as St. Nicholas but with no magic reindeer to help him out.

"One of the toughest areas to visit were the jungles of the Congo. One day, the Easter Bunny was doing a fundraiser for Easter Seals with Curious George, the famous monkey of children's books. George was curious as to why many of his friends in the Congo weren't getting their Easter eggs on Easter morning. When the Easter Bunny told him the problem, George said, 'Hey, maybe I can help you solve your problem.'

See no evil, speak no evil, eat no evil. The Easter Monkeys ponder life before the busy Easter holiday.

Solid chocolate Santas remind us of Clement Moore's Jolly Old St. Nicholas.

"It so happened that Curious George's sister was dating Grape Ape, the '70s cartoon icon, whose cousin used to hang out with the TV star, 'Lance Link, Secret Chimp,' who, in turn, was a pal to 'Chim Chim,' the monkey who pals around with Speed Racer's little brother, Spritle. Chim Chim had a friend whose brother's girlfriend's cousin just got laid off from the banana factory in the Congo because he was eating all the profits. This 'friend's friend's cousin' needed a job. The Easter Bunny got his carrot number, gave him a call, and said, 'Hey, I could really use your help. I'm having trouble getting my eggs delivered to the Congo, and if you'd be willing to do it for me, I'll hire you to deliver all the Easter eggs.' The Easter Bunny knew he could trust this monkey because he was fired for eating bananas, not eggs.

"So the monkey took the job, since it was the best offer he had received — actually the only offer — since no one in the Congo wanted to hire a banana thief. And, sure enough, when Easter season came, everyone in the Congo had their eggs on time!

"The Easter Bunny was so thrilled, because for the first time, he had no complaints on his voice mail from people in the Congo. He called the monkey and told him, 'You did a great job! I'm so proud of you for getting all the eggs delivered on time. You know I was so excited to hire you that I never even caught your name. What is it?'

"The monkey, proud of his accomplishments, humbly and simply said, 'You can just call me The Easter Monkey!'

CHAPTER 5: The Folklore of the Crown Candy Kitchen

"And that is how the Easter Monkey came to be. Every year, at Easter time, he helps the Easter Bunny deliver all the eggs to everyone in the Congo and beyond. That's how everything arrives on time so that everyone can celebrate the true meaning of Easter."

When Ezell reported this story, in the true oral tradition of folklore, all of St. Louis was looking for a replica of the Easter Monkey. Enter Crown Candy Kitchen.

Ezell had done several programs from the soda fountain at Crown Candy. He would celebrate some obscure holiday, like chocolate sauce day, and cleverly show how chocolate sauce could be used in our daily lives. Usually he improvised as he spoke.

These broadcast pieces are extremely popular throughout the St. Louis metropolitan area. Because they are not serious news, they give everyone a chance to laugh and relax for a few minutes before they start their day.

One day, Ezell mentioned that a person could get a chocolate Easter Monkey from Crown Candy Kitchen. They were being sold, he told his listeners, along with the many different bunny shapes. Immediately, the phones started ringing at Crown Candy Kitchen. Everyone wanted an Easter Monkey and needed to know prices, sizes and availability.

Fortunately, the Karandzieffs had access to a "monkey mold" and started pouring the Easter Monkey in their signature, fine milk chocolate. But production could not meet the demand in that first Easter sales period. Many more people, even from outstate Missouri, wanted more Monkeys than the Karandzieffs could produce.

The power of a folktale was not lost. St. Louisans had not forgotten the story. Every year at Easter time Crown makes dozens of these molds — one size only — and continues the tradition of the "Easter Monkey."

Ezell's story, and its eventual place in Easter lore, follows the typical migrations of the oral tradition. The story is anonymous in origin; exists in slightly different versions every time it is told; has ambiguous "friends of friends" in the details; is always orally transmitted, never written, in its delivery; relates to characters already recognized in popular culture; and has elements of iconic figures associated with holidays.

Most important for application of the story to Crown Candy Kitchen, however, is the appeal of the Monkey to the simplicity and innocence of childhood. It is connected to the Easter Bunny, whose legend everyone can tell. But somewhere in our consciousness, lost over time, is the meta-legend of the Easter Monkey. Just as Crown Candy Kitchen strives to preserve

Ron Elz, popularly known as "Johnny Rabbitt," has given his name to a popular malt at Crown Candy.

goodness and the clear values of yesteryear, so the Easter Monkey fits into its vision. One person relates the story to another who relates it to another who relates it to still another person, never speaking of an origin, but believing in the joy of the story, relishing the addition of this simple pleasure to a traditional holiday.

The nine decades of Crown Candy's steady mission is compatible with the appearance of the Easter Monkey. And Tim Ezell, as the traditional anthropological "griot," or storyteller, continues to smile.

Hot Fudge

The hot fudge that is used for the standard hot fudge sundae at Crown Candy is freshly made twice a week. The process is the same as that used when the store opened nine decades ago. It requires constant stirring of the ingredients in a large copper pot simmering over a gas stove. The oar-like stirring paddle must be maneuvered in a rhythmical pattern in order to incorporate everything consistently and avoid burning the mixture. Near the end of the process, the fudge sauce thickens and becomes more difficult to stir.

It is this thickening of the hot fudge sauce that created the lore. As the legend is told, during the '40s, a female customer who was eating a hot fudge sundae lost her dentures to the unforgiving sauce. After the dentures were retrieved and the woman consoled, it was decided that a disclaimer should be placed on the menu about the hot fudge. No one wanted a collection of dentures competing with the Coca-Cola memorabilia! So, to this day, almost 70 years later, the menu at Crown Candy contains the following warning: *Homemade fudge sauce, thick, hot and gooey, served over two scoops of ice cream, any flavor. Ask for the sauce separately if you like. WARNING: This is not for people with dentures!*

Johnny Rabbitt

Chapter 5: The Folklore of the Crown Candy Kitchen

Johnny Rabbitt Special

Ron Elz, a radio personality who goes by the moniker "Johnny Rabbitt," is an institution in the St. Louis area. Since the '50s he has served as a disc jockey, toastmaster, author and historian for the entire region. His programs, books and knowledge of St. Louis are unparalleled. If there were an ambassadorship of St. Louis, Johnny Rabbitt would be the logical and most popular choice.

It's only natural that Elz and Crown Candy have a history together. Elz's father was the owner of a drugstore in the St. Louis area. As in many other drugstores of the time, there was a soda fountain that served ice cream specialties. A signature for the Elz establishment was to add nuts, whipped cream and, finally, nutmeg to the malts upon request. Other fountains hesitated to add the nuts for fear they would harm the malt machinery. But Elz continued with his concoction and served many of his nutmeg malts before he sold his business.

Tommy, the caring animal lover of the Brothers Karandzieff, feeds Apache her breakfast.

Johnny Rabbitt dined at Crown Candy Kitchen on a regular basis. On one visit he ordered his "father's malt" instead of those on the menu. George Karandzieff, always eager to please a customer, especially the very popular Johnny Rabbitt, gave him what he ordered, and the rest, as they say, is history. Through word of mouth, the malt became so popular that Crown Candy decided to place it on the menu as the "Johnny Rabbitt Special." Thus was born a partnership. On his radio programs, Rabbitt would mention Crown Candy Kitchen and praise its ice cream, malts and candies. St. Louisans who had never been to Crown soon visited the place. The tradition was enhanced by the endorsement of the most popular St. Louis radio personality. And, after more than five decades, the Johnny Rabbitt Special is still a very popular malt.

The Common Man Customer

There is, in American folklore, a folk type known as the GOMER–the Grand Old Man of the Emergency

Crown's best-selling, legendary BLT sandwich made by Tommy (right), proudly states its benefits as well as the vision of Crown Candy.

Over the soda fountain, (far right) a sign warns people where to put their feet.

Room. These are people who frequent emergency rooms at hospitals with various minor illnesses — conjured up, of course, in order to feed their need for human interaction. Doctors and nurses can easily identify these "characters" and patiently deal with their idiosyncrasies.

This same folk legend can be applied to Crown Candy. For years, there have been regular customers who visit Crown for similar reasons. The lunches, ice cream, and candy are attractive, to be sure, but the welcome, the conversation of the wait staff, the banter easily overheard in the next booth, the sense of family, the absence of loneliness for at least an hour — all combine to keep these "grand 'old' people of Crown Candy" returning again and again. And everyone knows what their order will be before they give it.

Leo Berger, the "mayor" of Produce Row, was one of these folk characters. A large, jovial man who never knew an enemy, Leo visited Crown Candy daily, sat in the same booth, and ordered the same food — either a sandwich or an ice cream specialty on alternate days. Often, he would return in the late afternoon when the crowd was thinner and fall asleep in his favorite booth. And every Christmas, Leo would dress up in his Santa suit, mingle with the customers until his order was ready, and then return to his same booth and his same food.

Leo became like family, and on the rare days he missed coming to the store, people would ask where he was and worry that he was ill. His personality was so engaging and contagious that he became a permanent "grand old man of Crown." When Leo died, a plaque was inscribed to his memory and hangs near the booth that was his home away from home.

"Cabbage George," another GOMOCC (Grand Old Man of Crown Candy), may be the ideal folk type of this character — almost Runyonesque. He was a man of mystery who had no last name that anyone knew or

Sweetness Preserved: THE STORY OF THE CROWN CANDY KITCHEN

For more than 30 years, Bonnie Brogan (right) represented the spirit of Crown Candy with her down-home waitressing. She died an untimely death in 2003 and is remembered with a plaque.

that he would ever tell anyone. He frequented Crown as a friend of Uncle Pete Jugaloff and sometimes would help with odd jobs, but mostly just stand around and *kibbitz* with everyone. He meant no harm and caused none, but his stream-of-consciousness banter, his short stature, his off-the-wall observations, all created a one-of-a-kind character who deserved a nickname.

One certainty was Cabbage George's love for horse racing, which he shared in common with Uncle Pete. Together, they would frequent the tracks, never talking about their losses or wins, but making sure they scheduled regular visits to the "ponies." Many observers suspected that Cabbage George used code language that only he and Pete understood, since Pete, too, was adept at nicknaming people. But the truth will never be known, and that is the attraction of these folk characters.

No one knows what exactly happened to Cabbage George, but one day, he simply did not return to Crown

Candy. Pete had died before George, and for a few months, Cabbage returned but he was never the same. No one could contact him, and no one saw him again at the race track, but even today he is talked about in fond, humorous ways, as the "character of Crown."

There are residents of a nursing home, and seniors from an assisted living place, who come by the busload once a month and, like other regulars, order the same thing from the menu every time. Some of these customers were raised in the neighborhood many years ago and use these monthly visits to remember and reminisce.

There are the utility workers, the postal workers, the probation and patrol officers, and the delivery men who come in weekly, also order the same menu item every time, greet everyone in the store, and MUST sit in the same booth. This is their method of connection to an extended family.

Then there are the gospel singers who come in every Sunday, again order the same lunch and ice cream, and, by the way, sit in the same corner booth, even to the

CHAPTER 5: The Folklore of the Crown Candy Kitchen

point of waiting for it if it is already occupied.

And, also, there is Craig Mold's "gang," who can guarantee a yearly reunion at Crown Candy, complete with Dr. Seuss hats and joking memories of their own experiences at the soda fountain. On this yearly journey, the group includes all the customers already in the store in their revelry and invites them, in a familial way, to join in their fun. Their traditional lore expands, as does the meaning and attraction of Crown Candy.

All these "regulars" are Crown's "Grand Old Customers," who repeat the same phrases on every visit, order the same food every time, and represent a unique part of the folk history of the establishment.

The Ghost in the Back Room

There are several apartments above the Crown Candy store where many of the family members have lived over the years. These apartments are still there and occupied. But there was an additional apartment in the back of the store behind the candy-making room. This apartment is no longer there, but someone is. While making candy, over the years, employees have heard loud, moaning sounds from beyond the wall. There has been the occasional scream, also loud enough to be heard by the candymakers. No one knows any of the people who had ever lived in the back apartment. But the tales are still vital.

It seemed, as the legend goes, that before the Karandzieffs bought the building in 1913, various tenants had occupied the back room at different times. One spinster lady who had lived there the longest of the tenants — about 3 years — was found dead one day in this apartment. Her death was ruled a suicide.

Leo Berger, the "mayor" of Produce Row, in his usual mode of transportation.

When the Karandzieffs bought the building, no one was living in that back apartment and no one has lived there since. But at various times, the noise, the moaning, and the muffled scream, can be heard behind and through the wall. Whoever is making the candy at the time simply announces that the "moaning lady has returned." She has become a supernatural legend in the whole folklore of Crown Candy Kitchen.

1983: The Fire

It was December 25, 1983, at 7:30 in the morning. Many St. Louisans had celebrated Christmas the night before and opened their presents; others were sleeping, dreaming of Santa's arrival that very morning. The Karandzieff family had closed the soda fountain early on the 24th. It had been a successful Christmas season filled with chocolate Santas, angels and elves. Now it was time to enjoy the holiday as a family. But life intruded.

The space heater in the store's restroom malfunctioned and started a fire. Fortunately, the place was closed. The rear of the confectionery suffered the most damage. A portion of the original tin roof ceiling, some of the Coca-Cola memorabilia, one of the wooden booths and a section of the back wall were ruined by fire and beyond saving. Fortunately, firefighters had arrived very quickly and were able to save most of the history of Crown Candy.

Eyewitnesses still recall the "delicate manner" in which the fireman fought the fire. Several firehouses answered the alarm, and all of them were aware of the tradition of Crown Candy Kitchen. Working in the cold December weather, with the temperature below 0 degrees and a wind chill factor of 20 degrees below 0 on Christmas Day, they were inspired by the season to prevent needless destruction of the store. They succeeded in saving the soda fountain, all the original booths, most of the Coke collection and all of the equipment used to make the candy and ice cream.

Later on Christmas morning, more than 100 people came to Crown Candy to help with the cleanup. And on January 31, 1984, one short month later, Crown Candy Kitchen opened its doors again. The place had not lost any of its tradition or history. The partially burned tin ceiling was restored with pieces found to match the original. The back wall was replaced with similar materials, and the booth was reconstructed. Only the restroom needed a complete overhaul. And the story was reported on television stations around the United States.

The spirit that was Crown Candy survived unscathed and became stronger. The Karandzieff family, grateful for the assistance of so many, fully realized what "their place" meant to the community. After 70 years in the same location, their neighbors were not about to let history die on that Christmas day.

Chapter 5: The Folklore of the Crown Candy Kitchen

Neil Svetanics had been the beloved Fire Chief of the City of St. Louis for many years, and a regular patron of Crown Candy Kitchen. He was instrumental in saving Crown Candy in 1983. Customers continue to joke that Crown was saved because Chief Svetanics had a passion for the ice cream and could not bear to think of a life without it. So, in his honor, a sundae was created. But the sundae served as more than a "thank you" to Chief Svetanics. The Karandzieff family was grateful — very grateful — for the firefighters whose work, under the Chief, had saved the family's livelihood. They were very touched, moreover, by the response of the whole community, who believed that history had been preserved.

The Fire Chief Special is one of the most popular sundaes even today. It serves as a dual symbol: gratitude to the work of the often-underappreciated firefighters and recognition of the importance of the past in our present and our future.

Fire Chief Special: Two scoops of ice cream covered with chocolate sauce, strawberries and sliced bananas, pecans and crushed nuts, and a mound of whipped cream.

St. Louis Today; Tomorrow the World!

They did not seek it; it found them. Worldwide fame, award-winning confections, and a presence in the world all followed Crown Candy's dedication to quality in its product, care for its customers and consistency.

Crown Candy Kitchen has been the subject of countless stories in St. Louis media. It has been featured on CNN, the Food Network's "Food Finds," in *Gourmet Magazine*, *Bon Appetit Magazine*, *Money Magazine*, *The New York Times*, *The Chicago Tribune*, and *The Los Angeles Times*, among other publications.

The store itself has been used as a backdrop for fashion layouts, historical narratives and holiday features. The family's recipes have been recorded in books on the history of ice cream, the evolution of the sundae in America, and the origin of the banana split as an American icon. Entire radio programs on St. Louis stations have been broadcast from within the store's booths.

At Christmas and at Easter times, Crown Candy has shipped chocolates to every country in Europe, to Australia, South Africa, China and Canada, and to every state in the United States of America.

The Karandzieffs have designed custom chocolates for election campaigns; inaugural chocolates for Missouri governors; "thank-you" chocolate cards for St. Louis corporations; ice cream cones for 1904 World's Fair re-enactments; and numerous "designer" chocolates for wedding celebrations. They have even sponsored softball teams for the St. Louis Symphony Orchestra. On a regular basis, Crown Candy donates ice cream and chocolates to charitable fundraisers.

Soda Fountain Folk Vocabulary

Even though the owners of Crown Candy Kitchen tout the importance of things not changing in their establishment, one element of their tradition indeed has disappeared: the coded language of the soda jerk.

For years, a folk language has been used in many different vocations to serve as a bond for the craftsmen and to distinguish it from other jobs. Where the language developed is not known; anonymity is a hallmark of folklore. This language just developed and migrated among American soda jerks, who unconsciously were protecting their own turf. And it became traditional, existing in different versions in different regions of the country, but always understood by soda fountain workers.

The Karandzieffs were a family of immigrants from Macedonia who started the business with their craft. The language not only of America, but also of the soda fountain, was difficult, but it had to be learned properly for them to survive. So, initially, their language of conversation was broken English, which became a stronger American speech over time. They had no reason to import a special soda fountain vocabulary, which would create an unnecessary confusion.

However, when the family began to hire outside employees to meet the needs of a rapidly growing business, these "American" additions allowed for some small introduction of the folk language of the soda jerk. George and the "boys," who were second and third generation, respectively, were able to encode the folk vocabulary and understand what was being ordered. Most often, however, they declined to use it except in cases where its secrecy was necessary or purposeful.

Using it or not, the folklore of soda jerk speech became a part of American idiom and is still used today in various applications, even away from the soda fountain.

A "black bottom," for example, would be a chocolate sundae using chocolate ice cream. A "houseboat" is a banana split and references the shape of the bowl in which the split was served. If the fountain clerk were told to "hold the hail," he would not put ice in the glass. When something was "on wheels," it was an order to go. When he was asked to "shoot one," he knew he had to "draw" a Coke. Numbers were a big part of their lingo: yelling "95" meant a customer was walking out without paying his bill. A call of "86" meant that the item ordered was sold out, and no longer on the menu for the day. An "81" was a glass of water; and "82" was two glasses of

CHAPTER 5: The Folklore of the Crown Candy Kitchen

It's hard to beat Crown Candy's BLT and a chocolate malt for lunch.

water. Hearing the number "13" meant to be aware because the "big boss" was around. Presumably, the number refers to the traditionally bad luck associated with the number. When the owner was present, everyone had to be on their best work behavior. "I need a black and white" would be an order for a cup of coffee with cream. And whenever the term "burn" was used, it referred to a chocolate malt. "Burn" always meant a malt, and since chocolate was by far the most popular kind, only one word was needed. But you could "burn a van" for a vanilla malt, "burn a straw" for a strawberry malt, or "burn a ban" for a banana malt." If you "burn it all the way" you wanted a chocolate malt with chocolate ice cream.

This folk vocabulary was a delightful representation of a once very proud occupation. The language of soda jerks survives in the oral tradition, but the soda fountain is gone and has taken the language with it. At Crown Candy Kitchen, the "American" help used it briefly with the younger sons in the Karandzieff family, but it has outlived its usefulness. It's the one thing that has changed at Crown; but it did not affect the quality of the product, the high level of customer service, or the consistency of the food.

And all of the benefits from this lore have been accomplished without any budget for advertising or self-promotion. THE NAME of Crown Candy has been the object of an oral tradition in St. Louis for its entire 90-year history. It is a folklore unto itself. And, as with any lore, its stories exist in different versions, but all of them reflect the "goodness" of Crown Candy Kitchen. ♛

Sweetness Preserved: THE STORY OF THE CROWN CANDY KITCHEN

A Paparazzi Paradise

The importance of Crown Candy Kitchen to the St. Louis community cannot be overstated. Not only is it a place for good comfort food and great desserts, but also it serves as a meeting place for St. Louis politicians, media personalities, judges, sports figures, CEOs and "wannabes." Gossip columnists love Crown Candy because "everyone" goes there, and it saves them trying to find someone for a story. Many a deal has been brokered at Crown Candy; and to paraphrase the vernacular, "if those booths could talk," the St. Louis area might have a different history.

Many celebrities and ordinary people have given testimony to the importance of Crown Candy Kitchen in their lives.

Tim Dorsey, a well-regarded and respected radio mogul in St. Louis, is the Vice President and General Manager of KTRS (550 AM).

"First of all, my favorite lunch is a Crown Candy egg salad sandwich on white, a bowl of chili and the greatest chocolate malt in the universe.

"My first visit to Crown Candy would have been in the '50s with my parents. We didn't go often because it was an extra special treat.

"In the mid-'70s, I became a regular. I joined KMOX Radio (the CBS affiliate in St. Louis) in 1975, just a stone's throw, maybe a long punt, from St. Louis Avenue. The late and very great Jack Carney* reintroduced me to this restaurant, and for nearly 15 years at KMOX, I had lunch there once a week. Crown Candy is much more than the best malts, candy

A summit meeting of regulars at Crown Candy: George (far right) meeting with Mayor Vince Schoemehl, and friends, Messrs. Costello, Meyer, and Signaigo.

One of the many Coca-Cola trays at Crown. This special one is thought to be of one-time actress and singer Georgia Frontiere, now the owner of the St. Louis Rams.

Sweetness Preserved: **THE STORY OF THE CROWN CANDY KITCHEN**

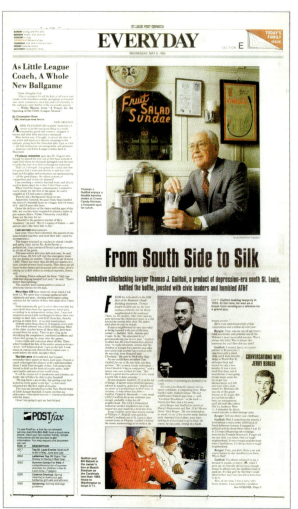

and lunch food in St. Louis. It's a kind of 'Cheers.' It's nostalgic, warm, friendly and simply full of character and integrity. It's pure in that it doesn't pretend to be anything more than it is — a great place to spend a half-hour for lunch.

"I haven't met many people as friendly and down-to-earth as George Karandzieff. George makes you feel like you're a warm friend coming into his home. My kids love Crown Candy mostly because of George and his family. They love the hot dogs and the desserts, but they really got a kick out of going behind the restaurant where George worked his magic — making chocolate anything. He'd work away and chat with the kids at the same time. He took an interest in them and made them feel welcome and important.

"I've had the pleasure of presenting five of my daughters at the *Fleur-de-Lis* Ball (an annual debutante soirée for the prominent Catholic families of St. Louis). We'd party the night away at a downtown hotel and the next day head straight to Crown Candy with the whole family (about 20 of us). That 'day after' at Crown Candy became a favorite family tradition, something our family will always remember and cherish…as we do Crown Candy."

Tom Guilfoil, Esq., is one of St. Louis' best-known lawyers and best interpreters of the City's history and politics. Known as a "lawyer's lawyer," he always took his trips to Crown Candy Kitchen in a limousine! He does not drive, so he does not own a car, but the symbolism of arriving in such style is intriguing. For Mr. Guilfoil, who was raised on the Near South Side in very humble beginnings, Crown Candy Kitchen represents the best of what St. Louis has to offer. He calls the family "grounded, humble, secure, visionary, ambassadors, self-effacing, honest, dedicated" and "damned nice people; the salt of the earth." Very often, Guilfoil, who is the lawyer for the former St. Louis Cardinals NFL team, now the Arizona Cardinals, would bring along in his limousine

*Jack Carney was THE radio personality in St. Louis for many years. The Karandzieff family credits him with much of their popularity, as he mentioned them on his program on many occasions. Carney died an untimely death from a heart attack on November 27, 1984, but is still very fondly remembered throughout St. Louis.

CHAPTER 6: *A Paparazzi Paradise*

NFL team owners, commissioners, even players to "this tiny establishment that represented St. Louis better than anything to me."

They would partake of the food and the ice cream specialties and were so impressed that when they returned to their home cities they would order Crown candies to be sent back to them. Guilfoil even admits to having serious discussions in a booth at Crown Candy. "After all," he says, "the food of our childhood could only help the negotiations. Anger could never follow a chocolate malt or some Heavenly Hash candy!"

Mel Carnahan**, Missouri's Governor from 1992 through 2000, used Crown Candy Kitchen on many occasions to campaign for the office. He used to come in just for a lunch, but couldn't resist the politician's opportunity to kiss a baby and shake someone's hand. There were plenty of each constituency built into the friendly crowd at Crown Candy, and Governor Carnahan was wise enough to use the opportunity to his advantage. But, very importantly, he felt that the BLT and chocolate malt were good enough reasons to visit Crown Candy Kitchen for lunch. In the end, his visits were always two victories — personal and public.

The St. Louis Post-Dispatch has used Crown Candy as the subject or backdrop of many pictures and articles. Here, Tom Guilfoil, Esq. (page 72) is featured enjoying a chocolate malt.

**Governor Carnahan died a tragic and untimely death on October 16, 2000, while he was campaigning for a seat from Missouri in the U.S. Senate. His plane, piloted by his son, Randy, crashed in a wooded area near St. Louis. The Governor, his son, and his Chief of Staff were all killed in the crash. Since it was too late to add another candidate to the ballot, Missouri law allows for the sitting Governor to name a replacement in the event the deceased candidate was elected. Indeed, Governor Mel Carnahan defeated then Senator John Ashcroft in the general election. And the appointed Governor, Joe Maxwell, named Jean Carnahan to take the U.S. Senate seat won by her husband, Mel.

Governor Mel Carnahan regularly visited Crown Candy as a campaign stop.

The Honorable Bob Holden, a career statesman and Governor of the State of Missouri from 2000-2004, visited Crown Candy Kitchen whenever he came to St. Louis. It became one of his favorite haunts. He recognized and understood the tradition and landmark status that Crown Candy held in not only in the City of St. Louis, but also in the State of Missouri and even nationally. In a tribute to Crown Candy's history, Governor Holden remarks that he "loves the food and the atmosphere, but most important is the fact that they stayed in the neighborhood during some very difficult times. Crown Candy is an institution in St. Louis. As citizens of the Show Me State, the Karandzieffs showed the world what small businessmen can do with a vision and a purpose. There was no need to super-size anything. Hard work, consistency of product, and quality customer service can make the difference."

For his inauguration, Governor Holden commissioned Crown Candy Kitchen to create a chocolate favor to commemorate the event. It was a fitting, compatible linking of what the best of Missouri can do and a reminder that traditional values can still operate in the speedy information age.

Governor Holden often made trips to Crown Candy when he was not on official business in St. Louis. For him, "the BLT and the chocolate shake are the perfect comfort food." And, he adds: "Our sons, Robert and John D., enjoy taking their friends to Crown Candy and giving them the tour of the back room where they make the candy. It is always a delight when George K. is working because he greets you with hands full of warm chocolate. This is nostalgia at its best."

In a related story that illustrates the "happenings" at Crown Candy, Michael Kilfoy, a St. Louis designer and

CHAPTER 6: *A Paparazzi Paradise*

illustrator, met Governor-elect Holden and his family in a chance encounter at Crown Candy.

"I used to take my kids there as a treat if they were good. My son, Sean, and I were sitting at a booth and I noticed the Governor was there; so I pointed him out to my son. Governor Holden noticed this and came over and introduced himself. We talked for more than 20 minutes! He was very down-to-earth, warm, and gracious. When he left to order, my son leaned over and said to me, 'So, where do you know him from?' as if I had known him for years!

A little later, the Governor sat at a booth next to ours and asked Sean what flavor malt he was drinking. Sean told him it was his favorite, chocolate marshmallow. The Governor said that it sounded good to him also and he ordered the same thing. I told Sean that he had just

aided the Governor in making his first executive decision! Crown Candy Kitchen really is the kind of place where things like this happen."

Frank Cusumano, a popular sports broadcaster on KSDK-TV, (Channel 5, the NBC affiliate in St. Louis), cites Crown Candy often in his broadcasts as he makes friendly wagers with listeners: "I'll bet you a chocolate banana malt from Crown Candy" as part of his story line. He, too, frequents the place:

"My favorite lunch is a BLT with a banana malt. But that doesn't compare with visiting George Karandzieff in the back room with my three kids. It's hard to forget his ability to make everyone feel special as he shakes hands with his chocolate-covered fingers. And watching him make his chocolate specialties, with all his humility, is a lifetime of memories in itself."

Governor Bob Holden often brought his family to Crown Candy, and even had Andy mold chocolate greeting cards for his inauguration.

Sweetness Preserved: THE STORY OF THE CROWN CANDY KITCHEN

George with friends, Don Costello, Johnny Rabbitt, and Chief Svetanics at a party in George's honor.

Tony's, in downtown St. Louis, is the City's only five-star restaurant and the perennial top vote getter in any survey of St. Louis' best restaurants. Founder, owner and chef Vince Bommarito is, importantly, an admirer of Crown Candy Kitchen:

"I lived in North St. Louis, which was a wonderful place to grow up. The many cultures — stable neighborhoods, strong parishes, and every neighborhood had its park. There were a lot of sports competitions that brought us to play Hoc-Soc at 'Neighborhood House' on occasion. After our games we went to Crown Candy and had malts.

"Years later, I went there with my wife, who lived a 'couple of neighborhoods' north of Crown Candy. We became friends over the years with the Karandzieff family.

"They have always been gracious when I brought my children to Crown Candy when they were growing up — in recent years I brought my grandchildren. I always enjoy visiting with the Karandzieffs. I guess because we are both in the food service business we have a special bond.

"We still buy their delicious malts! No one does it better."

Perhaps no greater tribute to the quality of the food at Crown Candy can be given than from Vince Bommarito, the "star" of St. Louis chefs.

State Representative Thomas Villa, who represents the 108th District in Missouri, comes from an established, well-known St. Louis political family who have devoted their lives to public service. He has his own praise for Crown Candy:

"Crown Candy provides a unique time warp that takes one back to a simpler time. I have been

CHAPTER 6: A Paparazzi Paradise

privileged to tour the making of the candy. The antiquity of the molds is in itself fascinating. FAMILY tradition is paramount at Crown. The family pride in the overall operation is refreshing. Ice cream sodas, made the way they should be, prove a unique experience at Crown. I really like the ham and cheese and egg salad sandwiches. Root beer floats reign! The interior is functional and works. The Crown Candy Kitchen is a virtual island of pleasure in a neighborhood that is still proud. St. Louis City can take a lesson from the Crown Candy operation. Keep it simple, be user friendly, and serve quality at a fair price."

Martin Duggan, the quintessential newspaper man, is the retired editorial page editor of the former *St. Louis Globe-Democrat* and now the venerable host-producer of "Donnybrook," on Channel 9, the St. Louis PBS affiliate. This very popular program features four St. Louis celebrities who are provoked by Mr. Duggan every Thursday night to produce a lively, entertaining and informative program. Here is what Martin Duggan has to say about Crown Candy:

"I learned about Crown Candy from a newspaper article in the 1960s and quickly became a regular customer. Having been a soda jerk during my high school days at The Penguin, an ice cream parlor at Oak Hill and Connecticut in South St. Louis, I have been a milkshake junkie all my life.

"What a treat to gulp a vanilla shake at Crown while munching a crunchy BLT with the right amount of bacon, followed by lots of black coffee.

"My loyalty to Crown was such that I made it a weekly ritual to go there on my lunch hour from the *St. Louis Globe-Democrat*, coinciding with a visit to the Pink Sisters Convent at Adelaide and Warne. I was most often accompanied by my dear friend and secretary, Florence Litwicki, who had known the Karandzieff family earlier.

"Proprietor George Karandzieff made us welcome in the kitchen when he was making special chocolate treats for Christmas and Easter. His sons, Mike, Andy and Tommy, always took care of us. The waitresses, Bonnie and the twin sisters, Tammy and Pam, were great.

"Through the years, I enjoyed bringing family and friends to Crown, especially those from out of town, to show off this delightful, nostalgic landmark.

"To this day a visit to Crown is a must for our daughter, Mary Leahy and her family, of Austin, Texas, when they are in town. The same is true for our son, Joe Duggan, from Washington, D.C.

"As a special penance during Lent, I would substitute a grilled cheese sandwich for my customary shake. That is REAL sacrifice! Just thinking about Crown makes me hungry for the end of Lent!"

Marty Hendin, the long-time public relations director of the St. Louis Cardinals Major League Baseball team, also has fond memories of Crown Candy:

"My favorite memory is getting to go into the back room and watch Mr. K. make Easter bunnies and other items. The sight, smell and taste — WOW! — one of life's great experiences."

The magnetic personality of George Karandzieff was special and a great memory.

Chief Joe Mokwa, the affable and charismatic Chief of Police for the City of St. Louis, is a frequent customer at Crown Candy Kitchen and has been for more than 35 years. He jokingly calls the place "his donut shop." "There is nothing free there," he quickly adds, "but the ambiance is so cheerful and inviting." Mokwa started going to Crown as a cop in the district and "I always buy a chili tamale and a chocolate malt." He adds that, for him, "Crown is 'Cheers!'" In the daily work of the policeman, Crown recalls for Mokwa an earlier time, when values were more clear and clean, and people greeted each other without hesitation. "Simply, Crown exudes joy, and that is something we all need."

Mike Owens, the investigative reporter for KSDK-TV and a native of St. Louis, has memories from high school that transferred to his profession:

"My oldest memory of Crown Candy is 'running' in that neighborhood in the late '60s with buddies from Holy Trinity Catholic Church. We went to the old DeAndreis High and sometimes hung out at Crown. There was a group of us, and a couple had hot cars, like a Malibu, and the other guy had a fast Dodge. Crown was a beacon of light for the area and for us.

"Fast forward to the '80s when I'm working in downtown St. Louis. I recall meeting George for the first time…big, husky, and always with a grin. He would offer to shake my hand, but his was covered with warm chocolate. It tasted good, but you could lose interest when you saw his big mitt with chocolate on it! George was always a great host and I would often introduce new folks to Crown by taking them back to the kitchen to meet the patriarch. It was a treat for me and my guests to get to the back room.

"But I never did like to eat in the kitchen, like some did. I was afraid I was missing all the sightings out front and the diversity of the crowds and waitresses, especially Bonnie."

One of the guests whom Mike Owens brought to Crown Candy was Cordell Whitlock, a reporter and anchor for KSDK-TV. Whitlock is not from St. Louis, but his perspective makes him seem like a native:

CHAPTER 6: *A Paparazzi Paradise*

"Shortly after I moved to St. Louis, colleagues took me to Crown Candy. I had to see the most important places first, so I was told! I ate a BLT and the homemade Oreo ice cream and I've been going back ever since. I've lived across the country, and it's difficult to find small, family-owned businesses still thriving. A big part of Crown Candy's appeal is not only the food but also the fact that you get to personally know the owners. Andy and the rest of the Karandzieff family have always been gracious, and stopping by the store is always a treat for me and my friends."

Al Wiman, was a veteran medical reporter for KMOV-TV (Channel 4, the CBS affiliate) for many years before he became the Director of Communications for Webster University in St. Louis. Al was a regular for lunch at Crown Candy for many years. When asked about his experiences, Wiman succinctly said:

"Going to Crown Candy is like going home again. For me it's like a looking glass and I see nothing but chocolate and it's wonderful. You can always find your past at Crown Candy, and with George at the helm you can be certain that it will be consistent and memorable. No eating establishment is more comfortable than Crown Candy. I have taken many people there and they have all returned on their own. It's St. Louis' gift to the whole world."

Joan Fann, an executive with the world-famous St. Louis Symphony Orchestra, has a great memory from her childhood about Crown Candy that became an integral part of her profession:

"My first recollection of Crown Candy Kitchen is when I was about 6 years old. My two brothers and I were picked up by our father after attending Sunday

Fire Chief Neil Svetanics has a sundae named in his honor at Crown Candy that commemorates the fire of 1983, when he "saved" the store.

Tony Curtis spends a moment with Bessie, our favorite leading lady.

School at the 4th Baptist Church near Crown Candy. Since we were so close to the place, as he reminded us, we should stop for something to eat. Our father would order a chocolate malt for himself and each of us. We loved the malts, but given our age, we were never able to finish them because they are so large, as you know. My father, who was a large man, would finish all the malts that we could not drink. And he warned us every time not to tell our mother we had been to Crown. But every time we sat down to eat our Sunday 'dinner,' which was a big thing back then, and served at 'lunchtime,' my mother would look at my father and say, 'Joe, you've taken the kids to Crown's again.' We kids, of course, told our father that we didn't tell her. For years we thought our mother was psychic. Only when I was older did I realize that she could tell we had been to Crown because we were picking at our food, her carefully prepared Sunday 'dinner.'

"As fate would have it, in my business career with the St. Louis Symphony, I had to entertain prospective sponsors by taking them out to lunch. These folks were from Chicago, New York, San Francisco…'sophisticated places.' I realized these people would be comparing our restaurants to their 'excellent' establishments. So I decided to take them, every time, to a place unique to St. Louis — Crown Candy Kitchen. George K. would give them a tour of his 100-year-old candy molds and as a gift a dozen or so of his chocolate-covered Oreo cookies.

"Always — within a day or two of visiting Crown — I would get a thank you letter and a request for more chocolate from George. They loved the place as much as any St. Louisan did!

"George K. was the force that kept Crown Candy going. He is a kind man who knows what his job is, without pretense, and who lives to return all his blessings to the community. For 12 years, Crown Candy sponsored the St. Louis Symphony girls' softball team and made sure we had treats to 'keep our strength up.' Little did George know that all those treats kept the weight on…but we never refused them!

"Five generations of my family have patronized Crown Candy Kitchen. For me it was as natural as going

CHAPTER 6: A Paparazzi Paradise

to church and keeping our father's 'not-so-secret secret.'"

But the "common man" was the real backbone of Crown Candy's patronage. The whole establishment, in fact, was a great leveler. The place had no pretense, and the customers were not expected to have any either. All were treated the same.

Bill Harrison, from San Antonio, Texas, is a typical example of the way Crown Candy has affected people's lives:

"I have no special events and happenings to share. What I do have is almost 60 years of experiencing pleasant, tasteful memories with several generations of my family and friends.

"In the '40s (Crown was already in business for more than 30 years) my parents introduced me to the Kitchen's delightful ice cream and candies. We did not live far from Crown Candy, and on a Friday or Saturday night it was our family treat to take a walk to get a malt or sundae.

"In the '50s Crown became my standard dating haunt that I shared with several young ladies, including my fiancée. It was always a highlight of the date.

"In the '60s, after I had joined the military, married and moved away from St. Louis, Crown was always included in all of my visits back home when on leave.

"In the '70s, it was my turn to share this time-honored establishment with my daughters when we visited St. Louis. We even went there before visiting the Arch!

"In the '80s and '90s, my business travels often brought me to St. Louis, and my fellow travelers happily tagged along. My English friends even took several chocolate figurines back to the United Kingdom with them.

"Now we're in the new millennium and I have brought my granddaughter to Crown to savor a chocolate malt as only the Karandzieffs can make them. My family even had a four-generation reunion at Crown's. There was my 94-year-old aunt, my wife and I, my daughter and her husband, and my granddaughter. All of us enjoyed this visit as much as my first time back in the '40s. Only the prices on the menu board above the back mirror have changed. The quality, quantity, and service have all remained the best in St. Louis."

Dr. John Oldani standing behind the real celebrity in this story: George Karandzieff.

And Judy Holmes of House Springs, Missouri, tells of her parents' experience with Crown Candy:

"For years my siblings and I have heard the stories of Crown Candy from our parents. They loved Crown Candy so much that in 1945 my father brought my mother there and asked her to marry him! She agreed and they were married in 1946, and have been married for 57 years.... They assure us today that the day of the proposal at Crown Candy was the greatest day of their lives and has the most memories. For their 50th Anniversary, friends of the family presented my parents with a framed artist's rendition of Crown Candy! Can I say that without Crown Candy my siblings and I would not be here today? We think so!"

Bob Laske of St. Louis has a continuing history with Crown Candy, also. But his became "fancier" over the years:

"I started going to Crown Candy in 1941 when I was 10 years old. I lived very close to the store, and my three cousins lived only one block away. So, every summer, from 1941 to 1948, we would spend two or three days a week there. We always went after 2:30 p.m., when the lunch crowd was gone. Malts were only 25 cents then, and a lot of times the four of us would split two malts. They still did it the same way back then. You'd get the glass plus the large metal container they made it in. In those days, money was scarce so we would sell newspapers or shine shoes so that we would have enough money for Crown Candy.... My wife and I still go to Crown once a month. The only change we can notice is that the coin-operated jukeboxes in each booth were not working. Everything looks exactly as it did in 1941, from the way they make the sundaes and malts to the Coca-Cola memorabilia all over the walls.

"In 1995, on our 40th anniversary, I surprised my wife. We went to a 4:00 p.m. Mass at St. Boniface Catholic Church along with my children and four grandchildren. Afterwards we went to my daughter's house where, at 5:00 p.m., a 10-passenger limousine picked us up, to my wife's great surprise! Guess where we went? To Crown Candy Kitchen for malts and sundaes! Afterwards the driver took us through Forest Park for a memory ride with our bellies full of delicious Crown Candy ice cream. There is no better way to celebrate a special occasion!"

Doris Reeves of St. Louis connects Crown Candy with World War II. She and her girlfriends would meet regularly at Crown where all the "guys" were.

"I can't begin to tell you how many teenagers met for malts at Crown Candy. It was one happy time. Harry Karandzieff and Uncle Pete never got angry with us; I'm sure they had reasons to be, but it never happened.

CHAPTER 6: A Paparazzi Paradise

They were the nicest people in the world. It was the summer of 1942 that I remember the most. Because the next year most of the young fellows joined the service; some were drafted and some were not even 18 years old. Friendships had been formed at Crown Candy, and while our boyfriends were overseas, Crown became a place for all of us girls to meet and bond; it was a haven from the war.

"And I can recall with great emotion the December of 1944, on a Saturday night, when the boys who had left returned as men to Crown Candy just as we had done in 1942. The place was jammed with men from every branch of the service. But, sadly, not all of the Crown regulars returned. We used the place to remember and to grow up too quickly.

"I know of at least 17 couples who met at Crown Candy who eventually married. Over the years we would meet at wedding receptions or, sadly, at funerals, and Crown Candy was always a topic of conversation. Many are deceased now, but those of us still here remember Crown Candy fondly as our 'haven from the world.' I have revisited the place many times, not as often as I would like to, but I shall never forget how welcome we were as teenagers trying to understand the world."

Throughout the comments of these primary sources, there are several enduring themes: comfort, nostalgia, simplicity, tradition, goodness. Yet connecting all of them is the overriding concept of equality. From the richest, most well-known St. Louisan to the common folks in town, everyone is treated the same at Crown Candy Kitchen, and no one ever forgets that courtesy. For one simple hour or even less time, Crown serves for everyone as a family or a home, where greetings are genuine and pretense is forbidden.

There have been no changes for more than 90 years at Crown Candy Kitchen, as many people recalled. But no one ever complains, because in this stressful, anxious, ever-changing world in which we live, time has stopped — incredibly! And when you visit this place, to paraphrase Robert Frost, "they take you in and celebrate who you are."

The prescription for whatever ails you: repeat visits to Crown Candy Kitchen in order to feel whole and good again. ♛

Sweetness Preserved: THE STORY OF THE CROWN CANDY KITCHEN

Some Sweet Stats

Americans are crazy for ice cream! They don't just "scream" for it; they "die" for it — the "flavor is so delicious, it's to die for." There's an old aphorism attributed to an American, anonymously: "Without ice cream, life and fame are meaningless." During World War II, for example, among uniforms, boots, rations, weapons, and tanks, the Government listed ice cream as "essential" for the troops. Ice cream fountains were even constructed on ships so that sailors could ease the stress of homesickness and war. And ice cream mixtures were even placed in the turrets of war planes! Ice cream became a positive intervention for stress and was equated with FUN. It even surfaced in the name "Good Humor," which added "motorized" ice cream delivered to your doorstep.

If chocolate is added to the equation and melted into "deadly" confections and sweets, arguably, the American pursuit of happiness is a road paved with "frozen butterfat" and lined with variations of "molded cocoa beans." The soda fountain and the confectionery become significant American institutions revealing much about the American character.

When Crown Candy Kitchen was established in 1913, there were several other confectioneries in the area. All of them were considered "good sized," all of them had their special clientele, and all of them prospered — for a time. Eventually, however, when ice cream and candy factories were built throughout the United States to produce the bulk products for easy sale in the emerging supermarkets, these confectioneries closed — except for Crown Candy Kitchen. But its size never changed.

Mike Ruggeri proudly displays some of the dozens of chocolate-covered strawberries that he prepares for Valentine's Day every year.

Sweetness Preserved: THE STORY OF THE CROWN CANDY KITCHEN

Joe Eisenbraun prepares a take-out lunch for a regular customer.

Behind the main dining area, which seats only 52 customers regularly, there is a small room, 5 x 7, where the ice cream is made. There is a kitchen with one prep table and one "hot counter," and a corner for take-out foods. Next to the kitchen is another small room where the salads are prepared. Behind this room is a packing room, where the candy boxes are filled and the candy molds are developed and "cleaned." And, finally, behind the packing room is a larger room, which runs the length of the store but houses the table and the slabs for making the candy, the chocolate melting tubs, and the line-up of the various candies, tilted on wooden sorting shelves. A small 4 x 6 office is at the end of the long room. That's it.

Crown Candy Kitchen is not a large establishment in size. The mass production and marketing of ice cream and candy throughout the United States has not made it obsolete. The fact that it has thrived unchanged for almost a hundred years underscores the astounding appeal of a soda fountain and the value it can provide.

For an establishment that seats so few comfortably at any one time, the number of raw materials needed to serve all the customers, or the amount of ice cream sold monthly, or the pounds of candy sold yearly, tell dramatically, in numbers, the tradition, the landmark that is Crown Candy. In their 90th year it has arrived at a level of "pantry" that was only a dream in 1913. Every year the logistics are greater and "sweeter."

Consider the raw materials:

16,000 pounds (8 tons) of chocolate used yearly to make the specialties

900 eggs boiled each week for the popular egg salad

800 ice cream cones ordered each week

720 buns consumed each week

700 pounds of bacon fried each week for the heart-stopping BLT

500 hot dogs sold each week

400 pounds of sugar used monthly

320 16-oz. bags of potato chips opened each week

300 pounds of tomatoes sliced each week

200 loaves of bread opened each week

CHAPTER 7: Some Sweet Stats

180 pounds of chili cooked each week (without beans)

180 heads of lettuce cleaned weekly

160 pounds of corn beef sliced each week for the Reuben sandwiches

130 gallons of ice cream sold every day

125 pounds of bananas peeled weekly

105 pounds of turkey sliced each week

75 large cans of whipped cream squirted each week

70 pounds of ham sliced each week

56 pounds of tuna used each week for the tuna salad

50 pounds of pickles used weekly for sandwich garnish

50 gallons of soda pumped weekly

50 pounds of buttered, roasted pecans opened weekly

40 pounds of cheese sliced weekly

30 pounds of whole chickens boiled for the two days that chicken salad is made and served

25 pounds of onions diced weekly

18 gallons of chocolate syrup poured weekly

17 pounds of marshmallow topping used weekly

15 pounds of sauerkraut used each week for Reuben sandwiches

13 gallons of caramel syrup cover sundaes weekly

9 gallons of pineapple topping applied weekly

6 gallons of homemade hot fudge used/made weekly

5 gallons of mayonnaise opened weekly

4 gallons of cherries used weekly for sundae toppings

In summer, fresh peach ice cream is added to the menu and in winter, egg nog ice cream is produced. These require more raw products on a seasonal basis.

In this amazingly small establishment, these staggering numbers demonstrate, in a very convincing manner, how greatly people need and cherish the magic of Crown Candy Kitchen. Ice cream and chocolate can provide clues to our American character. ♛

Todd Goebel spreads the homemade thousand island dressing on the ever-popular Reuben sandwiches for the luncheon rush crowd.

Sweetness Preserved: THE STORY OF THE CROWN CANDY KITCHEN

Crown Candy Recipes

"**Preserving the goodness**" serves as a dual motto for Crown Candy Kitchen: the goodness of the past, synonymous with the innocence of youth, where American values and family structures were eminently clear, and the "goodness of taste" of the ice cream, candy, and lunches, which must never be compromised.

As a corollary to their motto, one can often hear the three brothers, while, in a moment of rare "madness" discussing strategic planning for the store, saying: "Change is not good!" And the strategic planning is complete, at least for another year, when the results will be the same.

However one needs to argue with these mantras, the success of Crown Candy, for more than 90 years, cannot be disputed. It has flourished incrementally every decade.

The lunch's biggest seller, by far, is the BLT…better known as the "heart-stopping-BLT" with the added description: This is NOT a health food store! After 90 years, Crown Candy is still defiantly maintaining its "old time stick-to-your-ribs" menu items. In fact, the method of frying the bacon is a family secret, used for all these decades. The result is a distinctive flavor to the bacon not matched anywhere. But here's how the BLT is made:

Put 12 pieces of bacon on white, wheat, or rye toast; slather it with mayonnaise; add lettuce and tomatoes…you have the comfort food of all comfort foods, at least at Crown for 90 years.

Every week, Andy prepares (far left) the very popular peanut clusters in the dipping room surrounded by Coca-Cola collectibles.

Bessie and George (left). George has always considered Bessie his recipe for success.

Sweetness Preserved: The Story of the Crown Candy Kitchen

A view from behind the antique candy counter, with the traditional "penny" candy alongside the homemade chocolates.

If you are not in the mood for a BLT, try their egg salad or chicken salad or tuna salad or Reuben. Or chili. Or a chili dog! They are all family recipes where, again, no change is allowed. And there are 23 different soups, two made daily, and frequently rotated.

But given all these sandwich/lunch choices, the dessert specialties, with 14% butterfat ice cream, are the essence of Crown Candy Kitchen. There are a variety of choices, all from among three definitive categories identified with the Americana soda fountain: Sundaes, Newports, and Deluxe Sundaes. Stubbornly holding on to these standard offerings, Crown offers the Sundae: ice cream and syrup — nothing else; or the Newport which adds nuts and whipped cream to the sundae; and the Deluxe, which adds more flavors of ice cream and syrups to the basic sundae.

Crown Deluxe Sundae

The Crown Deluxe Sundae is the biggest seller among the specialties and it, by itself, serves as a metaphor of the entire ethic of the store. It is really not unique; it is really not very beautiful; it is not big on the current presentation qualities — but eating this sundae is very close to a "religious experience." Each one is made with real vanilla ice cream topped by homemade hot fudge and caramel sauce, covered with butter-roasted pecans — REAL pecans! — and every bit of it oozing into a synergy that is close to perfection. It takes a real understanding of what is required to make a sundae — and Crown has perfected it. There is not one spectacular part to it, but together is becomes the best of 90 years. There is childhood, happiness, goodness, memories, nostalgia, a pleasant past — a veritable time warp — in every bite.

French Sundae

The adjective "French" is used here because Harry Karandzieff and Uncle Pete Jugaloff wanted to add

CHAPTER 9: Crown Candy Recipes

some "international flavor" to their desserts in order to accommodate the many immigrant groups who had moved into the neighborhood. Italian, Polish, Jewish, or German as descriptions for sundaes just did not quite conjure up a dessert delicacy, and, since there were few French immigrants in the area, the owners felt that no one of the larger groups would be offended if their nationality was not chosen. So French it was, and Crown Candy called it "elegant" and "sweet" and the perfect dessert uniting some unusual but tasteful flavors. It continues to be a big seller 90 years later.

Want to make it?

Take a large ice cream dish, oval shaped, and place two scoops of vanilla ice cream in the middle. Slice a banana in pieces and surround the ice cream with it. Then take 2 oz. each of strawberry, pineapple, and marshmallow sauces and ladle them over the ice cream. Cover the whole dessert with whipped cream, a handful of real, crushed, toasted cashew nuts, a handful of chocolate sprinkles, and top it off with a cherry. French in the title or not, this is a sweet, elegant dessert.

Uncle Sam Sundae

This ice cream specialty, created by Mike Karandzieff, won an award in a national competition of sundae creations from various ice cream stores throughout the United States. It's an *homage* to the American icon who represents Crown Candy's roots and gratitude for what America has given to the Karandzieffs.

If you want to be patriotic while eating your ice cream, make this sundae. Take a wide, oval-shaped bowl, put two large scoops of vanilla ice cream in the bowl and drown each scoop with strawberries and pineapple sauce. Add chopped bananas and whole butter-roasted pecans. Smother the whole creation in whipped cream and top it with a cherry.

One would expect that with the name "Uncle Sam," there would be variations of red, white, and blue ice cream or flavors. Not for Crown Candy! For them the name follows the use of the most popular American ice cream flavor: vanilla; the most popular American fruit toppings: strawberries and bananas; and the surprising

Marshmallow Easter Eggs are boxed and ready for Easter baskets.

use of an unusual topping to represent the American colonial symbol of welcome: the pineapple! Here is the most "American" of sundaes for Crown Candy. And when all the flavors meet, the "melting pot" becomes one delicious tribute.

Hot Fudge Banana Split

The banana split, made in its traditional American way, is a popular creation at Crown Candy. But the homemade hot fudge sauce that the Karandzieffs make weekly was too good to be placed only on a sundae. Why not marry the delicious sauce with the All-American soda fountain creation? So Harry, Uncle Pete, and George began offering the Hot Fudge Banana Split, with two scoops of ice cream, preferably chocolate, placed in a long, narrow, boat-shaped glass container, with two banana slices placed around the ice cream, covered with a large ladle of hot fudge, a mountain of whipped cream, topped with a cherry and a generous coating of toasted crushed cashews to make a decadent dessert. With the American love of chocolate as comfort food and the historically significant banana split so united, this creation now outsells its traditional parent.

Desserts to Drink

In addition to the many ice cream specialties, Crown Candy continues to serve many drinks associated with the American soda fountain. There are phosphates, which use seltzer water with many choices of flavors. Or the ice cream soda, which uses seltzer water, ice cream, and, again, many choices of flavors. And the classic Float, which uses ice cream and a soda, like root beer or orange. But the champion of all "drinkable" desserts is the Malt.

Some say the whole reputation of Crown Candy is built on this specialty. They are all 24 ounces, mixed in original metal containers, in the two-bladed malt machine, with 3 large scoops of ice cream, fresh whole milk, and old-fashioned malted milk power. Served in the same frosty container in which they were mixed, the malts come in several flavors, with chocolate, again, being the favorite over the years. Adding a fresh banana to the malt is a very popular combination and makes some guilt-ridden customers feel as though they are at least getting their potassium in this calorie-laden, hypnotic, creation.

The biggest appeal in consuming these drinks is being surrounded by the Coca-Cola memorabilia covering the walls, and imitating the painted couples sipping the same malt through their straws, in their time of innocent flirting. It becomes a worry-free exercise, where the world has stopped, and your grandparents are, once again, alive and you can know what "good" really is.

CHAPTER 9: *Crown Candy Recipes*

'THE' Chocolate

If, after a BLT washed down with a chocolate banana malt, you still have room left for candy, your choices are limitless and difficult. Heavenly Hash is the biggest seller and the signature creation of Crown Candy, but its recipe, like all the candies, is carefully guarded. Just think of marshmallow, thickly covered in milk or dark chocolate, and generously topped with chocolate covered, butter roasted pecans. The taste sensation, the synergy of all the elements, is received on different levels: the smooth marshmallow, the creamy chocolate, and the pecans all have a taste separate from the whole, but when combined, create different taste experiences that define the "best" seller without any words.

Nut clusters — pecan, almond, cashew, or macadamia — are also made daily, as they have been for decades, and continue to be best sellers.

Old-fashioned peanut brittle, molasses puffs, coconut clusters, chocolate covered caramels, "snappers," almond bark, chocolate-covered fresh strawberries or just plain broken chocolate, milk or dark, are among the many choices given to the customers.

One candy creation or an assortment can be packed in gift boxes from one-half pound to five pounds — even eight-pound, heart-shaped boxes on Valentine's Day.

And if these chocolate specialties aren't enough, there are the time-honored licorice whips, or giant jaw breakers, or jelly beans, or taffy and other confectionery candies that Crown continues to stock as necessary artifacts to an American confectionery.

There are no calories in memories, and no cholesterol in nostalgia. Have one of everything! ♛

The Santa mold and crates await their appointed duties on the workbench in the backroom at Crown Candy.

Sweetness Preserved: THE STORY OF THE CROWN CANDY KITCHEN

Curious Queries and More!

Over the more than 90 years that Crown Candy has been in business, thousands upon thousands of customers, obviously, have entered the establishment and ordered from the menu. And with one major focus of Crown, customer service, being drilled into each employee, there's bound to be many examples of stories, folk tales, legends, and even folk vocabulary experienced or overheard by Crown's personnel. The wait staff enjoys their discourse with the customers and is practiced in a saintly patience. Even when the crowds are lined up out the door and around the side of the building, no one is rushed or hurried to get out. Because a large part of the experience of a visit to Crown is the interaction with the people in a booth next to yours or a conversation with the waitress or soda jerk, questions about "a history" or product are legion. To paraphrase a popular culture phrase: customers ask the darndest things!

Here are some examples of customers' concerns expressed over the years:

What does a vanilla malt taste like?

Do you use real bananas in your banana splits?

If I order a malt, will I get it cold?

Do you cut your BLT sandwiches into two or three parts? I can only eat two!

I'll have a cheeseburger. (We don't serve them.) OK, then I'll take a hamburger. (Crown Candy has never served hamburgers or French fries.)

What does your egg nog ice cream taste like?

Can you ship an ice cream cone to my daughter in Oregon?

Sometimes there's barely time to catch your breath. A busy day during the lunch hour at Crown Candy (far left), and **Jerry takes a moment** to greet a customer.

Sweetness Preserved: THE STORY OF THE CROWN CANDY KITCHEN

Tammy picks up a couple of BLTs just prepared by Tommy for the hungry lunch crowd.

Is your bacon beef?

What's a BLT? (The waitress describes it.) Oh! So there's no meat in it!!

Do you use real chocolate in your candy?

Do you have someone who carves out each of those chocolate Santas?

If I order a banana split without bananas, what do you call it?

Who is Uncle Sam? (A customer was asking about the name of a sundae.)

Do you grow your own bananas?

Is it cheaper to eat in here or take it out?

Does your black walnut ice cream have pecans in it?

What are cashews?

Do you make ice cream during the winter?

Why do they call it a Reuben? Was he the owner of the store?

Do the eggs for your egg salad come from chickens?

Do you put ham on your chef salad or do you use real meat?

There are no beans in your chili. Does someone take them out every day?

Is the breaded chicken white, rye, or whole wheat?

Why do they call it horehound candy?

If I order a BLT, a tamale, and a bowl of soup, will I have room for a banana split?

Do you have indoor plumbing here?

Why are your nuts fifty cents more?

Is a malted the same as a malt?

Do you use red tomatoes?

If I order an extra egg on my chef salad does it come soft or hard boiled?

Why are your wooden booths so hard?

Do you have to melt dark chocolate like you melt light chocolate?

What did you do before the store opened in 1913? (Asked of a waitress in 1995)

Is your ice cream made from yogurt?

Do you grind the coffee beans before you put them in the coffee ice cream?

How hot is your hot chocolate?

CHAPTER 10: *Curious Queries and More!*

Can you pick out just the red jelly beans for me? I need two pounds!

Does your sugar-free candy cause diarrhea?

Do you pay for people to use the parking meter?

Will you put money in the parking meter for me or let me know when I need more to put more money in?

Did you guys invent ice cream?

Why is it called a sundae?

How long does it take an ice cream cone to melt?

Which ice cream sundae will not give me brain freeze?

Can I have a spoonful taste of every one of your ice cream flavors before I decide which one to buy?

Do you put lettuce in your salads?

Why do you call your ice cream "black cherry?" Aren't cherries red?

There are no answers to most of these questions, but they do, at the same time reflect the history that is Crown Candy and the interest that people have in something hallowed. The "wonder" of the unchanged, unique confectionery allows for this illogical but respected banter.

A Sweet Quiz

Here is a look at more direct questions.

The manufacture of ice cream and candy in the United States has grown to more than a ten-billion dollar industry and increases every year. America has an unrivaled sweet tooth. But how much do you know about either product? This quiz will determine if you deserve a treat!

1. What is the biggest holiday for candy sales in the United States?

2. In what country was milk chocolate invented?

3. What country has the highest *per capita* consumption of candy?

4. Which President designated July as National Ice Cream Month?

5. What are the top 5 most popular flavors of ice cream?

Sam, Tommy and Timmy celebrate the 4th of July in style.

The antique ice cream flavor board, which rarely changes.

6. On which day of the week is most ice cream purchased?

7. Which 3 cities in the United States purchase the most ice cream on a *per capita* basis?

8. Approximately how many licks does it take to finish a single-dip ice cream cone?

9. Where and when did the first ice cream parlor open in the United States?

10. In what city in the U.S. was the "sundae" invented?

11. Who invented the first Valentine's candy box?

12. What percentage of Americans prefers milk chocolate over dark chocolate?

13. What country is the largest producer of cocoa beans?

14. In what year did Milton Hershey introduce the first Hershey milk chocolate bar?

15. When did the Baby Ruth candy bar first appear and for whom was it named?

16. What is the #1 selling candy bar in the United States?

17. When were Marshmallow Peeps introduced?

18. What does NECCO, as in Necco Wafers, stand for?

19. When did Hershey Kisses make their first appearance?

20. What country produces 80% of the world's vanilla beans used to make ice cream?

21. Where was the first commercial ice cream plant established?

22. Who is usually credited with making the first frozen dessert?

23. Ice cream in the U.S., at more than $2 billion in sales yearly, is topped in sales by only one other dessert. What sells more than ice cream?

24. What 3 countries consume the most ice cream?

25. Which state in the U.S. produces the most ice cream?

CHAPTER 10: Curious Queries and More!

Answers

1. Halloween
2. Switzerland
3. Denmark, at 29.5 pound per resident
4. Ronald Reagan in 1984
5. Vanilla, chocolate, butter pecan, strawberry, Neapolitan
6. Sunday
7. Portland, Oregon; St. Louis, Missouri; and Seattle, Washington
8. 50 licks
9. New York, 1776
10. Evanston, Indiana
11. Richard Cadbury in England in 1868
12. 65%
13. The Ivory Coast in West Africa
14. 1900
15. 1920, and named for President Grover Cleveland's daughter, Ruth
16. Snickers
17. 1954, in the shape of little chicks
18. New England Confectionery Company
19. 1906
20. Madagascar
21. Baltimore, Maryland in 1951, by Jacob Fussell
22. Emperor Nero of Rome using snow, fruit pulp, and honey
23. Cookies, at more than $4 billion in sales
24. United States, New Zealand, and Denmark
25. California

Scoring

21-25 correct: You should consider donning an apron and joining the frontlines at Crown!

16-20 correct: Maybe you could work the fountain.

11-15 correct: You are certainly a junior *aficionado*.

6-10 correct: You need to stop by Crown more often.

1-5 correct: You must not have much of a sweet tooth.

0 correct: You've got to get out more! No ice cream OR candy for you! ♛

Tommy K. in the packing room, wrapping Heavenly Hash for Valentine's Day.

Sweetness Preserved: THE STORY OF THE CROWN CANDY KITCHEN

Afterword

As **Crown Candy Kitchen** approaches its 100-year anniversary, it continues to serve as a popular mirror of society, reflecting the innocence of the past and the happiness of an earlier, simpler life. Gaze into that mirror, and grandfather appears; or perhaps a first date, an anniversary, the "gang" from high school — or a youth not jaded by the excesses of "affluenza."

Crown Candy Kitchen is a tangible, working, living symbol. It calls us to a common history and a common tradition. People return to the old soda fountain to rekindle memories. They revere it as if they are on a pilgrimage to a sacred shrine of their childhood. It helps to define their character as Americans in ways that are always pleasant, worry free and stable.

While eating a BLT and drinking a large chocolate malt, one instantly knows what is valuable, good, and important. Customers return again and again for these cherished values. They can become "centered" and forget the blinding speed of the world outside. The years of accumulated dust on the soul can be whisked away with a visit to Crown Candy. The ice cream creations say hope. The chocolates say happiness. Together they say we can survive.

Comfort is the effect of the Crown Candy product. It has been around, unchanged, for almost 100 years. Yet, in this speedy age of information, and with less time to "smell the roses," one cannot help but try to predict the future of Crown Candy. Once the three brothers have reached their self-imposed retirement age — as yet undetermined — there is no one after

Andy K. prepares to deliver his special order.
The old German molds (left) of the Easter Bunny and St. Nicholas will soon have another chocolate life.

Sweetness Preserved: THE STORY OF THE CROWN CANDY KITCHEN

Denice Chaffin picks up a hot order from Tommy K. during the busy Friday lunch hour.

them in the family who will take on the traditions of the business, along with the necessarily very long workdays, seven days a week.

Crown Candy Kitchen is in the unique position of being a destination landmark in the middle of Old North St. Louis, which, like many other communities, has experienced significant physical blight and decay. A recent, dynamic neighborhood association has been established and has aggressively scheduled house tours, rehab tours and historical tours of the area. And the University of Missouri-St. Louis Public Policy and Research Center recently has conducted a survey among patrons of Crown Candy Kitchen in order to discover the depth of the "anchor" of Crown to the revitalization process. More than 900 patrons responded to questions designed to aid UMSL in providing answers to their proposal:

★ Who is visiting Crown Candy Kitchen?

★ How long have they been coming to Crown Candy?

★ What is the perception of the Crown Candy's patrons of the neighborhood around the eatery — the past five and the next five years?

★ How do Crown's patrons reconcile their perceptions of the neighborhood with their obvious fondness for the restaurant?

★ How does exposure to Crown Candy impact perception of the neighborhood's past and future?

CHAPTER 11: Afterword

★ How does the identity of Crown Candy change the way that the neighborhood is "read?"

★ How does Crown Candy influence local revitalization opportunities?

★ What is the significance of Crown Candy and its impact upon patrons for the local revitalization process that has been happening in the neighborhood of Old North St. Louis?

The results are not strategically conclusive, but directive and positive. And since St. Louis has always aggressively promoted its neighborhoods, there is a cautious optimism that Old North St. Louis will return. In what form, only time will tell. One conclusion from the survey, however, was very apparent: as a destination landmark and attraction, Crown Candy Kitchen continues to grow at an amazing rate. Ninety years has not diminished its appeal.

Crown Candy Kitchen will continue to be kind of a living history museum, serving the same fare, in the same way, to some very familiar faces and even to some new "historians." But in the distant future — some decades out — Crown Candy may be only a memory. And, not just a memory, but an image of all that was good. And it will still make us smile. ♛

Craig Mold and his gang of friends pose for their yearly reunion. They return to their "house of worship" and reminisce.

Sweetness Preserved: THE STORY OF THE CROWN CANDY KITCHEN

Appendix: The UMSL Study

Crown Candy Analysis and Summary of Findings

Survey Conducted by the Public Policy Research Center at the University of Missouri St. Louis

Published in 2004

The University of Missouri–St. Louis Public Policy Research Center sponsored a survey of patrons of Crown Candy Kitchen, a landmark ice cream and candy eatery located in the Old North St. Louis neighborhood. Conducted in the winter and spring of 2003, the survey asked patrons to fill out cards while visiting the establishment. In the first phase of the survey, approximately 1800 survey cards were completed; the analysis completed here is based upon the first 970 responses.

1. Zip Code of Respondents

★ The respondents were spread across a number of Zip codes. The numerically largest respondent group is from the 63107 Zip Code (the Zip Code to the north of Crown Candy); however, that represents only 42 responses, or 4% of the total sample. 5% of the respondents were from the neighborhood (63107 and 63106).

★ One-quarter of the respondents were from the City of St. Louis; 90% of respondents were from the Missouri portion of the St. Louis Metropolitan Area.

★ Besides Zip Codes in the immediate area, other high responding Zip Codes include south St. Louis City, the central corridor of the City, Affton and Oakville in south St. Louis County, University City and Clayton, Webster Groves, and

An early promotional clock by the makers of **Whistle Soda** that hangs near the ceiling at **Crown Candy Kitchen**.

The Parks Building across the street from **Crown Candy**.

Kirkwood in inner West County, and Florissant in north St. Louis County.

★ With the exception for the 63107 Zip Codes, the high responding Zip Codes are mostly white or integrated, of middle or middle-low income.

★ Respondents were largely long-time visitors (41% for more than 10 years) or first-time visitors (17%). Fewer respondents were short-term visitors (9% for less than 1 year) or medium-term visitors (14% for 2 to 4 years).

★ Most visitors to Crown Candy are local visitors. 95% of the respondents indicated that they traveled less than 50 miles, with 75% traveling less than 20 miles. 50% of the respondents traveled less than 15 miles, with 25% traveling less than 6 miles.

2. Perception of Past Change of Crown Candy Block

★ Crown Candy is in the unique position of being a destination landmark in the middle of a community that has numerous signs of physical decay and blight. Over the past several years, there have been signs of redevelopment in the area, but it is unclear whether those signs are visible to visitors to Crown Candy. It is also unclear to what extent visitors' experience at Crown Candy shapes — the assumption being that the experience of Crown Candy is generally positive — their perception of the neighborhood.

★ The largest category of respondents (43%) thought that the area had stayed the same. The balance of the other responses is skewed to a more positive perception than a negative perception. 35% of respondents felt that the area had gotten somewhat better, with 9% thinking that the area had gotten much better. Only 15% thought that the area had either gotten somewhat worse or much worse (2%).

★ There are small, but statistically significant differences in the perception of the blocks around Crown Candy, based on differences in the respondents. Some of these differences in perception are largely driven by resident proximity to Crown Candy. Thus, the perception of the blocks around Crown Candy worsens as the distance traveled to Crown Candy increases. Residents of Zip Codes closer to Crown Candy have generally higher, better perceptions of the blocks around Crown Candy than those who live further out. Respondents who come from Zip Codes with higher median family incomes have slightly worse perceptions of the blocks. Respondents who come from Zip Codes with larger populations of African Americans have slightly better perceptions of the blocks around Crown Candy.

★ The perception of past change on the blocks around Crown Candy worsens as the exposure of the respondent to Crown Candy increases. Thus, those who have been visiting Crown Candy for more than 10 years have a slightly worse perception of the blocks than those who have been visiting less than a year.

★ Most categories of respondents have more or less the same mean perception — between the perception that the blocks around Crown Candy have "stayed the same" and that they have become "slightly better."

3. Expectation of Future Change of Crown Candy Block

In general, respondents were more positive in their assessment of the future prospects of the blocks around Crown Candy than their perception of the past. One-half of respondents thought that the area would get somewhat better, with 21% thinking that

APPENDIX: *The UMSL Study*

the block will get much better. 22% thought that the block would stay the same, with only 7% thinking that the block will get either somewhat worse or much worse. Respondents from the City of St. Louis are more optimistic than those from outside the City. In general, respondents have more favorable attitudes about future change than past change.

4. Preferences for Other Establishments

⭐ 66% of respondents thought that the area should have another restaurant. This reflects the fact that most respondents come to the area to eat at Crown Candy, and have no other association with the area — as a shopper, resident, or worker. Similarly, 55% of the respondents indicated a coffee shop. 40% of residents thought that the area should have a grocery; this is surprising given that only 5% of respondents come from the area around Crown Candy. 24% indicated the desire for a pharmacy.

5. Dates and Times of Visits

⭐ Anecdotal evidence suggests that Crown Candy is busiest at lunchtime; the survey found that only 35% of the respondents indicated that they visit during lunch. The perception is slightly higher for weekday visitors than for weekend visitors. A slightly higher percentage of respondents visited on weekdays than weekends (51% to 49%).

6. Conclusions

⭐ While a majority of respondents had neutral to positive assessments of the neighborhood, there are differences based upon patron characteristics. Are these significant for the types of customers attracted to Crown Candy? Are the patrons most attracted to Crown Candy those who are most positive about the community and its future?

⭐ Patrons of Crown Candy are "smart" consumers of local visual cues. Do they notice the incremental steps that local residents notice — rehabbed housing, demolition of vacant eyesores and construction of new housing? Unsure. Anecdotally, there seem to be differences between the ratings of the neighborhood and the comments provided by respondents. Positive ratings of the community do not mean that respondents are not critical.

⭐ The context of Crown Candy may shift how the neighborhood is read, although probably not as expected. The fact that the first-time visitors have more positive rankings of neighborhood's past and future indicates that Crown Candy provides a richer sense of how the community is understood — for the context of Crown Candy — than just one of broken windows. 👑

Index

B

Berger, Leo, 62, 65

Bommarito, Vince, 76

Brogan, Bonnie, 18, 47, 64

Burgoon, Tom, 48

C

"Cabbage George," 62-64

Carnahan, Governor Mel, 73-74

Carney, Jack, 71-72

Chaffin, Denice, 18, 34, 50, 56, 102

Channing, Carol, 23

Coca-Cola memorabilia, 16, 35, 60, 66, 82, 92

Corner, Jim, 54

Costello, Don, 71, 76

Crown Candy Kitchen Fire of 1983, 66-67
    "Ghost of the Back Room," 65-66
    "Jeopardy!" appearance, 53
    Malt-drinking competition, 53-54
    Publicity in national media, 67
    Specialities of the House:
    Chocolate Malt, 22, 53-54, 92
    Crown Deluxe Sundae, 90
    Easter Monkey, 57-59
    Fire Chief Special, 21, 67
    French Sundae, 90-91
    "Heart-Stopping" BLT, 35, 62, 69, 89
    Heavenly Hash, 93
    Hot Fudge, 60
    Ice Cream, 90
    "Johnny Rabbitt" Special, 60
    Nut Clusters, 93
    Snappers, 36, 93
    Uncle Sam Sundae, 91-92
    Statistics (consumables), 86-87

Curtis, Tony, 80

Cusumano, Frank, 7, 12, 18, 75

D

Doherty, Warren, 54

Dorsey, Tim, 18, 71

Duggan, Martin, 18, 77

E

Easter Monkey (the), 53, 57-60

Eisenbraun, Joe, 86

Ellis Island, 25, 26

Elz, Ron ("Johnny Rabbitt"), 18, 60, 61, 76

Ezell, Tim, 18, 57, 60
    Story of the "Easter Monkey," 57-60

F

Fann, Joan, 19, 79

Frangoulis, John George, 54

Frein, Steve, 54

G

Goebel, Todd, 18, 87

Guilfoil, Tom, 72, 73

H

Harrison, Bill, 19, 81

Hendin, Marty, 77

Holden, Governor Bob, 18, 73, 75

Holmes, Judy, 19, 81

J

"Jeopardy!" 53

"Johnny Rabbitt" (See: Elz, Ron)

Jugaloff, Pete, ("Uncle Pete"), 13, 17, 28, 31,

INDEX

34, 39, 40, 43, 45, 48, 54-57, 64, 82, 90, 92
    Bond with Andy, 43
    Death, 94
    Friendship with "Cabbage George," 64
    Ghost of, 56-57
    Partnership with Harry, 28
    Semi-retirement, 39
    Taffy and fudge expert, 54
    "The Stare," 55

K

Karandja, Stanko and Christina, 26

Karandzieff, Andrew (Andy), 17-18, 28, 34, 41-45, 47, 89, 101
    Master chocolatier, 43
    Ombudsman, 45
    Sees "ghost" of Uncle Pete, 56
    Special relationship to Uncle Pete, 43

Karandzieff, Aristicia, 31

Karandzieff, Bessie, 18, 36, 37, 39, 41-42, 80, 89

Karandzieff, Eleni (Helen), 30, 33

Karandzieff, Emily, 41

Karandzieff, George, 9, 12, 17-18, 25, 27, 30-31, 35-48,, 71-72, 74-81, 89, 92
    Greeting visitors with chocolate-covered hands, 12
    Learning the business, 35
    Marriage to Bessie Di Polito, 36-37
    Retirement, 45
    Service during WWII, 36
    Takes over the business, 37, 39

Karandzieff, Harry, 13, 17, 25-28, 30-31, 33-35, 37, 39-40, 45, 48, 50, 54, 82, 90, 92
    Death, 45
    Emigrates to America, 26
    Establishes Crown Candy Kitchen, 27-28
    Expands Crown Candy business, 33
    Marriage to Aristicia, 31
    Marriage to Eleni (Helen), 28-29
    Partnership with Pete Jugaloff, 28
    Semi-retirement, 39

Karandzieff, Heather, 42

Karandzieff, Jenna, 42

Karandzieff, Laura, 42

Karandzieff, Michaela, 41

Karandzieff, Michael (Mike), 18, 39, 40-41, 45, 47, 54-55, 77-78, 85, 91
    As chocolatier, ice cream maker and display designer, 40-41
    Growing up in the business, 40

Karandzieff, Nancy, 41

Karandzieff, Neumo, 26, 30

Karandzieff, Ryan, 42

Karandzieff, Sherri, 45

Karandzieff, Thomas (Tommy), 18, 39, 41, 42, 45, 47-48, 55, 61-62, 76-77, 96-97, 99, 102
    Caretaker to neighborhood cats, 42, 61
    Takes over the kitchen, 41

Karandzieff, Tina (Athena), 19, 30-31, 35, 39, 41

Karandzieff, William (Billy), 31

Karandzieff Family Genealogy, 29

Kilfoy, Michael, 4, 19, 74, 110

Kranz, Natalie, 18

L

Laske, Bob, 82

Lee, Francet, 54

Lefevre, Richard, 54

Litteken, Bill, 54
Litwicki, Florence, 77

M

Macedonia, 7, 26, 30, 51, 68
Magee, John, 48
Mardirosian, Pam Goebel, 18, 47-49, 77
Martinez, Mike, 54
Moeller, James, 54
Mokwa, Joe (Chief of Police), 18, 78
Mold, Craig, 19, 65, 103, 110

O

O'Brien, Patrick, 54
Owens, Mike, 78

P

Plaque of Honor (for malt-drinking contest), 53-54

R

Rabbitt, Johnny (See: Elz, Ron)
Rall, Pastor Ron, 54

Reeves, Doris, 19, 82
Reynolds, Doug, 54
Ruggeri, Mike, 85
Ruth, Babe, 23

S

Sadowski, Rose, 50
Schlueter, Charles, 27
Schoemehl, Vince, 71, 73
Siebels, Tammy Goebel, 18, 47-50, 77, 96
Soda Jerks, vocabulary of, 68-69
St. Louis Symphony Orchestra, 68, 79
Steffan, Robert, 54
Svetanics, Neil (Fire Chief), 18, 67, 79

T

The Twins (See: Siebels, Tammy and Mardirosian, Pam)

U

"Uncle Pete" (See: Jugaloff, Pete)
University of Missouri-St. Louis Public Policy and Research Center, 102-103, 105-107

V

Villa, Thomas, 76
Vondras, Mark Matthew, 54

W

Whitlock, Cordell, 78
Wiman, Al, 79

ABOUT THE AUTHOR

Dr. John L. Oldani holds a Ph.D. in American Studies from Saint Louis University. He has been a professor at several American universities, directing American Studies Programs and specializing in American folklore. He has been featured on regular radio call-in programs on American Folklore for more than 30 years in St. Louis, Boston, Los Angeles, Chicago, Phoenix, and New York. Dr. Oldani was the writer for Johnny Cash's radio program, *AMERICAN FOLKLORE*, and has had a syndicated newspaper column, *AMERICAN FOLKSAY*. He has been inducted into the Great Teacher Hall of Fame and has received numerous Professor Excellence Awards. He lives in St. Louis with his wife, Carollee, and their three married children. Along with his two grandchildren, Crown Candy's Heavenly Hash and Black Cherry ice cream give great meaning to his life!

Uncle John with his two great-nephews, Adam and Dominic Key, continuing their own family tradition and having a great time at Crown Candy.